Book 1
Circuit Engineering
By Solis Tech

&

Book 2

Human-Computer Interaction
By Solis Tech

Book 1
Circuit Engineering
By Solis Tech

The Beginner's Guide to Electronic Circuits, Semi-Conductors, Circuit Boards, and Basic Electronics

Circuit Engineering: The Beginner's Guide to Electronic Circuits, Semi-Conductors, Circuit Boards and Basic Electronics

Table of Contents

Introduction

I want to thank you and congratulate you for purchasing the book, **Circuit Engineering: The Beginner's Guide to Electronic Circuits, Semi-Conductors, Circuit Boards, and Basic Electronics.**

This book contains a beginner's course on circuit engineering. Here, the basics of electric and electronic circuits are discussed. You will grasp the definitions of circuits, semi-conductors, resistors, inductors, transformers, circuit boards, and electronics, in general. You'll even be introduced to electrical safety tips and a set of skills needed in electronics, as well as a short take on reverse engineering, hacking, microcontroller programming, and robotics.

Alongside, you can apply all that you'll be learning once you get started with the proposed circuit projects for beginner. You'll also be rewarded a peek at different career-advancement possibilities. While reading about the fundamentals and various theories in the subject is important, hands-on learning is equally important. This way, you can put your newly gathered knowledge to good use.

If you're uncertain whether or not you have what it takes to learn the ropes in circuit engineering, let this book help you decide. Chances are, you have the stamina for the field and for all you know, you can discover a new passion for circuits and electronic devices.

Thanks again for purchasing this book; I hope you enjoy it!

Chapter I – First Things First: An Introduction to Circuit Engineering

In 1882, there was a *circuit war*; it was between the notable electrical engineers and scientists, *Thomas Edison* (inventor of the DC system) and *Nikola Tesla* (inventor of the AC system).

While Thomas Edison stated that an efficient way of distributing power was via a *DC system*, Nikola Tesla argued that although DC systems are efficient, an *alternating current* is the *more practical* option. It started as a simple clash of ideas, but it eventually led to a major rift. Neither professional conceded; both of them insisted that their own systems were "better".

In the end, it was *Nikola Tesla* that took home the *glory*. Case in point? He was granted funds by an internationally recognized firm, Westinghouse. The majority of the power sources of New York City were based on the ideas of the Serbian engineer; at Niagara Falls in Canada, a power plant was built.

If you're interested in finding out more about the particular *circuit war, AC and DC systems*, and all critical discussions on circuits, taking a course about electronic circuits is the way to go.

I.A. - What Is a Circuit?

Both an *electric circuit* and an *electronic circuit* refer to a complete pathway for electric current, which starts and ends at a single point; it is a passage that allows the electricity to enter at one place, then, let it pass through a series of stops, and finally, leave it to exit at the same place. The list of basic examples of a circuit includes a *light switch* (off and on) and *battery-operated lamps*.

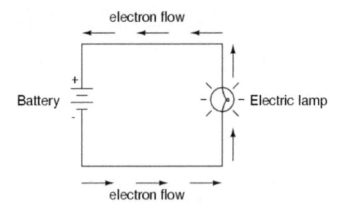

A circuit that follows a fundamental design

A circuit can function well - granted that its design is well-conceptualized. As much as possible, it is recommended that arriving at a simplistic product should be the goal; the simple and straightforward a design is, the better. With a fundamental concept, even if other (beginner-level) circuit engineers who will subject it to inspection will not have a difficult time in understanding its flow. Although there may be complex systems, the agenda is not intended to complicate the explanations.

Moreover, a circuit can be referred to as a space with a conductive path that grants electrons the opportunity to move freely. To create one with a brilliant design, a tip is to learn about the classifications of all circuits. You can use the knowledge to determine the appropriate kind of network, as well as the need for an external or internal source.

2 classifications of a circuit:

1. Linear or non-linear – a circuit that is based on either linear or non-linear networks; it is composed of independent and/or dependent sources and passive elements

2. Active or passive – a circuit that is based on either the absence (passive circuit) or the presence (active circuit) of a source; a source can be a power source or voltage source

I.B. - A Circuit & Its Types

Not all circuits are alike. In fact, one of the most common misconceptions involves an *electric circuit* and an *electronic circuit*; both are said to be one and the same, but they are not. While the former can carry *average to high voltage*, the latter has the tendency to have *low voltage load*.

Moreover, it is always important to be aware of the different circuit types, especially if you're about to make your own circuit; the kind of circuit that you create needs to have the ability to handle a preferred load.

Circuit types:

- Closed circuit – it is a circuit that is fully functional

- Open circuit – it is a circuit that can no longer function due to a damaged or missing component, or a loose connection

- Short circuit – it is a circuit that comes without a load

- Parallel circuit – it is a circuit that connects to other circuits; it is like the main power source or the primary circuit in a series of circuits

- Series circuit – it is a circuit that connects to other circuits; the same amount of electricity is distributed to each of its component circuits; the main power source or the primary circuit is unclear

I.C. - Conductors, Insulators & Semi-Conductors

Conductors, insulators, and *semi-conductors* give light to the fact that a circuit's electrical properties are dependent on the circuit type, as well as on their conduction bands (i.e. their allowed electric power). For instance, if a particular power source chooses to distribute a 9-volt electric power to a closed circuit, its electrical properties can be evaluated by using 2 details: (1) its characteristic as a closed circuit and (2) 9-volt electric power.

Moreover, conductors, insulators, and semi-conductors are integral concepts to the *conductivity* of an object. While conductors and semi-conductors are grouped to describe *charged carriers*, insulators are still considered as relative despite not containing any free charge.

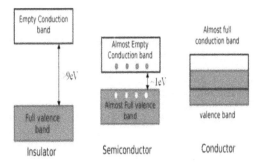

Insulators can be any "ion-less" object; the most common examples of semi-conductors are copper and aluminum & for conductors, gold and silver

Conduction bands:

- Conductor – it is a conduction band that is referred to as the almost full band

- Insulator – it is a conduction band that is referred to as an empty band

- Semi-conductor –it is a conduction band that is referred to as an almost empty band

I.D. - Breaking Down the Components of a Circuit

A circuit can be either *simple or complex,* and be both *simple and complex.* If the circuit in subject is a series circuit, with a group of 10 different circuits that are connected to it or if the said circuit is just a basic closed circuit with 5 different stops, it can be rather confusing to trace. However, if you dissect any circuit, you'll discover 3 *constant,* integral components.

Integral components:

1. Load – it is the representation of the power consumption, as well as the work that is accomplished within a system; without it, there's barely a point in having a circuit

2. Power source – it is where the electricity comes from

3. Pathway – it is the framework of a circuit; from the power source, it follows the load through each of the network, and finally returns to

and exits the power source; it is also referred to as the conductive pathway

I.E. - The Roles of Current, Resistance & Voltage

Current, resistance, and voltage are the 3 representations of the important components of a circuit's system. They can explain how electricity enters, then, moves from 1 point to another, and finally exits. Whether the path of electricity is rather simple, these representations remain constant. Apart from describing the electric flow, they can serve as indications of faults (in instances when a circuit fails to work).

3 representations:

- Current – it is the representation of the electric flow; particularly, its focus is on the flow of electrons

- Resistance – it is the representation of the nature of an electric flow as it moves around the circuit

- Voltage – it is the representation of the electric force or pressure; in general, the supply comes from an electric outlet or a battery

I.F. - AC/DC Systems: Which System Is in?

AC and DC systems (or alternating current and direct current systems) are often associated to each other. When the *AC system* is mentioned, so is the *DC system*. Conversely, when it's the DC system's turn to be in the spotlight, it won't be long until the AC system is mentioned. This is because these systems are opposite of one another; to get a better understanding of one of them, it's recommended to be familiar with the other, as well.

Moreover, *AC and DC systems* are types of a circuit's current flow. In an AC system, the current flow changes its direction occasionally. Meanwhile, in a DC system, the current flow follows a single direction.

It can be deduced, therefore, that an AC system grants a circuit freedom to let the current flow in several directions. While this can be an advantage, this doesn't permit the continuous flow that a DC system can entitle.

So, should you use an *AC system* or a *DC system*? The decision as to which current system is dependent on the more practical design to follow; take into account the aim of having your own circuit. If you prefer something grand and you intend to power something large, the AC system can step in. On the other hand, if you're good with a basic setup, you can use the DC system's concept as basis.

I.G. – What Is a Transformer?

A *transformer* is a device that serves as a portal for energy transfer within the points in a circuit or from circuit 1 to circuit 2. In most cases, it is used for increasing and decreasing the voltages in a system.

When the first transformer was built in the mid 1880s, circuit engineers discovered that a transformer significantly improves the electric flow in a circuit, and consequently, results to a more powerful circuit. The discovery made way for various transformer designs, as well as various transformer sizes.

A primary principle of a transformer is its need for extremely *high magnetic permeability*. It follows that a circuit that is capable of attracting power is, of course, more inclined to have electric current transferred to it; and, conversely, a circuit with *low magnetic permeability* is less likely to extract power from another circuit.

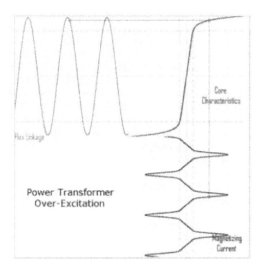

Magnetic permeability is defined as the ability of a circuit to hold and support an internal magnetic field

Chapter II – The Anatomy of a Circuit

Let's say that a lamp in your room has been around for a while, and let's say it chose to give up on you the other night; although it's an old lamp, you still believe it can *work fine*. You suspect that the problem is in the switching board. Instead of just letting it be and since you're interested in how it works, you choose to study its components.

As you open its internal system, you see that connected to some sort of panel are 2 wires; one wire is red, the other is black. As far as your knowledge in circuits can tell you, the 2 wires in your hands are: (1) a live wire or the wire that is connected to a switch, and (2) a neutral wire or the wire that carries the load.

As the universal rule in circuit engineering goes, *red* is the color that indicates a live wire, *black*, on the other hand, is a neutral wire. For a chance to know why your lamp gave up on you other than old age, checking the red wire would be a good start.

II.A. – Individually Speaking: Parts of a Circuit

A circuit can *work smoothly* if its individual parts are contributing to the workflow as expected. Remember that it follows a series; if one point in that series is not in condition. So, if you're wondering why a system is functional, check each one of its components. To use the old adage (and modify it a bit), the circuit, as a whole, is just as good as its individual parts.

Individual parts:

- Capacitor – it is in charge of the stability in the power source in a circuit

- Diode – it is in charge of supplying the light in a circuit

- Inductor – it is a coil of wiring system

- Resistor – it is in charge of power consumption

- Transistor – it is in charge of the electric signal control

II.B. – Circuit Categories: Which Category Do You Belong to?

Circuit categories describe the *voltage levels*, as well as their *electric flow over time*; they refer to how much and how powerful the current is as it enters and passes through each point in a circuit. Since they vary, it's listed as an effective way of understanding circuit systems of sorts if they are categorized.

Circuit categories:

- Analog circuits – these are the categories of circuits that use the concepts of parallel circuits and series circuits as basis. Among their fundamental parts are capacitors, diodes, resistors, and wires.

  In diagrams, analog circuits are easy to recognize. Usually, when a model of the particular circuit is drawn, a simple illustration is presented since these circuits do not follow a complex system. In most cases, when illustrated, the parts (e.g. capacitors, diodes, wires, etc.) are represented by lines.

- Digital circuits – these are the circuits that rely heavily on Boolean algebra (i.e. values are either true or false, or as denoted 1 or 0); therefore, these circuits are often dependent on transistors that can create closed logic. Compared to analog circuits, these follow a state-of-the-art design.

  Furthermore, digital circuits are designed to create either numerical or logical values for the representation of electricity that flows within their system. Since these are not only focused on the mere ability to take in electric current, but rather, on the individual properties of all of their parts, as well, these circuits come with advanced functions; they can provide memory and accomplish arbitrary computations.

- Analog-digital – these circuits are sometimes called hybrid circuits or mixed signal circuits since both system designs of analog and digital circuits are given light. Although their concept can be quite complex, these circuits can deliver a more thorough result; the procedures are combined, which allows collaborative effort from different parts. One example is a telephone receiver; first, it works based on analog circuitry to create and stabilize signals, then, based on digital circuitry, these signals are converted into digital units, and finally, are subjected to interpretation.

II.C. – Where Does Inductance Enter the Picture?

In circuit analysis, the term *inductance*, introduced in 1886 by *Oliver Heaviside*, refers to the property of a circuit's electricity-producing component to change in amount. Apart from the support of a circuit's aspect to vary, it points out the need for a filter and energy storage systems to be provided.

As it follows, the component in a circuit that enables inductance is called an inductor. Usually, these parts are made out of wire. But, while some circuits contain inductors as integral parts, others remain functional without the need to alter the electric flow.

Inductance can be either *mutual inductance* or *self-inductance*. The former refers to a change in electric current from one inductor to another inductor; it explains the primary operations of a transformer. Meanwhile, the latter refers to the *stable inductance* within a system.

Moreover, inductance is represented by the symbol *L*, which is meant to giver to the scientist, *Heinrich Lenz*. It also measured in units of *henry* after the American scientist, *Joseph Henry*; it follows that although it was Oliver Heaviside who introduced the term, the man behind the development is Joseph Henry.

Mutual inductance describes the occurrence in a circuit when there is change that can be traced to an inductor; particularly, it refers to the alteration due to an inductor's preference of a nearby inductor. It is essential to learn about the relationship of 2 *inductors* since it is the basis of the operations of a transformer. Additionally, a limit has to be maintained in order to keep potential energy transfers regulated; the failure to incorrectly calculate mutual inductance can result to *unwanted inductance coupling*, as well as a *power overload*.

It can, therefore, be deduced that mutual inductance (as represented by the symbol *M*) is the measurement of the coupling that involves 2 inductors; the 2 inductors are, then, given particular importance (in terms of coil turns), along with each inductor's ability to admit current flow or *permeance*. The formula for calculating mutual inductance is as follows:

**representations: M_{AB} = mutual inductance in circuit A and circuit B

N_B = inductance in circuit B

N_A = inductance in circuit A

P_{AB} = permeability in circuit A and circuit B

$M_{AB} = (N_B)(N_A)(P_{AB})$

When explained, the formula highlights that the mutual inductance between inductor A and inductor B (or M_{AB}) is equal to the product of 3 elements: [1] the coils of inductor B (or N_B), [2] the coils of inductor A (or N_A), and [3] the permeance of inductor A and inductor B (or P_{AB}).

On the other hand, self-inductance refers to voltage induction of a current-carrying system in respect to the changing current in the circuit. It points out that eventually, there will be another current that will flow along with the primary current. Due to the amount of force within the magnetic field, voltage is induced; particularly, voltage is *self-induced*.

II.D. - What Makes an Integrated Circuit?

An *integrated circuit* (or IC) is alternatively called a microchip or a chip, due to its size. It works depending on a particular signal level. One example is the integrated circuit that enables a computer to perform a multitude of tasks; instead of loading a computer's structure with a large circuit, it comes to the rescue.

In most cases, an *integrated circuit* operates at little defined states. Compared to the normal circuit whose operations are distributed over continuous amplitudes, it can function within a small network; the normal circuit may sometimes fail to work with only minor amplitude ranges.

Basically, an *integrated circuit* is no different from any other circuit; its power can astound you, yes, but, if it comes down to describing how it is, it's simply a circuit that has been reduced so it can fit inside a chip.

Chapter III – Resistance Isn't Futile

Without a material that can act as the opposing force, a circuit can *function*, but it may not function *as desired*. When an electric supply can perform its function by distributing electricity to the opening of a circuit, the electric current will keep on flowing; its flow can be uncontrollable, which can destroy a system's integrity. Usually, without the opposition, a circuit ends up taking too much load.

The term for this opposing material is *resistance*; it goes hand in hand with the term conductance. And, as mentioned in the first chapter, it is the representation of the current flow in a circuit.

III.A. – What Is Resistance?

Resistance is the measurement of an opposing electric current; it can be expressed in ohms. It generates an amount of friction that is relative to the necessary amount of electricity that a particular circuit can handle.

In a way, *resistance* is responsible for the *smooth flow of electricity* in a circuit. Although others would counter the argument by saying that rather than support the effortless flow of electricity in a system, it slows it down.

However, it is *resistance* that allows *balance of electricity* in a circuit. Take for example the case of a circuit that can only handle a total of 15V. If a circuit takes in 20V at a resistance of 5 ohms, the number is diminished to 15V, which indicates a functional circuit. Conversely, if, in the same situation, there is no *resistance* of 5 ohms, a circuit may not be as functional as desired; its system ends up carrying 20V, which implies that it is overloaded.

III.B. – Resistive Circuit 101

A *resistive circuit* is a kind of circuit that consists of nothing but a series of resistors to complete the combo of electric current and voltage source. If viewed in a chart, it is noticeable that the power waveform is always positive; it is suggestive the power in a circuit is always dissipated, and is never returned to the original source.

It is important to note that the frequency of the power in a circuit should not be equal to the frequency of the electric current and voltage. If possible, the frequency of the power should be twice as high as that of the electric current and voltage. This unequal frequency distribution grants constant change within a system.

Since it is made up of resistors and does not include transistors and capacitors, a resistive circuit is rather easier to analyze. Understanding the electric flow within the circuit (whether in an AC or DC system) requires a straightforward technique. Therefore, determining the flow of the current in a resistive circuit is simple; by adhering to the formula, calculating the figure is easy.

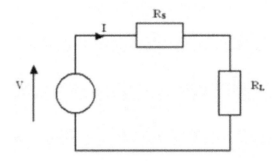

In a resistive circuit, voltage can easily be monitored

**representations: I = total current

RS = Resistance Source

RL = Resistance Load

I = voltage ÷ (RS +RL)

III.C. - War between the Types of Resistance

Resistance is classified according to the type of resistivity that it can contain, along with the amount of resistance that a circuit can carry. This allows the opportunity for an opposing force to be valued, regardless of its resistivity. As the professional electrical engineers can attest, not every circuit component that produces resistance satisfies the rules, particularly, *Ohm's Law.*

2 types of resistance:

- Differential resistance – it is the resistance derivative of voltage in light with the electric current; also referred to as *incremental resistance, small signal resistance, or dynamic resistance*, its concept is responsible for oscillators and amplifiers

- Static resistance – it is the resistance that corresponds to the typical definition of resistance; it is also called *chordal resistance* or *DC resistance*

III.D. - Resistance vs. Conductance

The average circuit comes with both *resistance* and *conductance*, which gives balance to the electric flow in a circuit's system. While the former refers to the opposition, conductance describes the amount of current that is converted into power that revolves around different points.

Conductance also covers the ability of a circuit's components to conduct electricity. And, to bring light to its counterpart's ability to oppose the flow, it dwells on the subject of the convenience of electricity to pass through a series of points in a circuit.

With both the resistance and the conductance in the system, a circuit can function as desired.

III.E. – The Need for Calculations (Four Ways)

For electric current to flow smoothly within a system, a level of resistance has to be present. And, since not all circuits come with a similar design, their resistance levels vary. To calculate a particular circuit's resistance, first, you need determine its type, and its provided values, as well.

Four ways:

#1 – Resistance calculation for a series circuit

The formula:

Resistance = $_1R +{}_2R +{}_3R +{}_4R$

#2 – Resistance calculation according to voltage & power

**representations: total voltage; PT = total power

The formula:

Resistance = $VT^2 \div PT^2$

3 – Resistance calculation according to voltage & current

**representations: VT = total voltage; IT = total current

The formula:

Resistance = VT ÷ IT

\# 4 – Resistance calculation according to power & current

**representations: PT = total power; IT = total current

The formula:

Resistance = PT ÷ IT

III.F. – What about Sheet Resistance?

Sheet resistance refers to the measurement of the resistance in a thin sheet in a circuit's components. It can be used to describe the resistibility of different circuits and can point out the specific difference in circuits that vary in size. Especially in the case of a commercial product, the topic is covered for the assurance of quality.

You can look at *sheet resistance* as a special kind of resistance since it generates a more specific value. Usually, the average resistance in a circuit is expressed in *ohms*; *sheet resistance* is expressed in *Ohms per square*.

In most cases, *sheet resistance* is used for the analysis of circuits with uniform conductivity or semi-conductivity. Typical applications are extended to quality assurance for a commercial circuit.

III.G. – The Role of Impedance & Admittance

Like resistance, *impedance* can be described as the opposition in a circuit; unlike resistance, however, it refers to the opposing force of a circuit after the application of voltage. It is only relevant to AC systems or circuits where direct current isn't the supplied.

It was in 1893 when the concept of *impedance* was initially introduced by the Irish engineer, Arthur Kenelly. Back then, it was denoted by *Z* and is defined as a complex number.

When it comes to quantitative terms, *impedance* refers to the ratio of voltage to the electric current in a circuit. Its introduction is important for beginners especially if they're scratching their heads as to why there's an opposing force besides resistance.

Impedance, like resistance, comes with values. In a single open circuit, its value is presented in *ohms*. In the event of a series circuit or a parallel circuit, its value can be calculated by simply adding all the defined values in each unit.

The formula:

Circuit Engineering: The Beginner's Guide to Electronic Circuits, Semi-Conductors, Circuit Boards and Basic Electronics

**representations: TZ = total impedance

Z_1 = impedance in component 1

Z_2 = impedance in component 2

Z_3 = impedance in component 3

Z_{10} = impedance in final component of a circuit

$$TZ = Z_1 + Z_2 + Z_3 \ldots Z_n$$

Meanwhile, *admittance* is a relative concept in circuit engineering. It addresses the issue that alongside the difference in the magnitude of the electric current and voltage that are flowing within a circuit, the difference in phases needs to be given light, too. This way, the maximum load within a system can be calculated accordingly.

The formula:

**representations: TY = total admittance

Y_1 = admittance in component 1

Y_2 = admittance in component 2

Y_3 = admittance in component 3

Y_{10} = admittance in final component of a circuit

$$TY = Y_1 + Y_2 + Y_3 \ldots Y_n$$

Chapter IV – It's Time to Measure the Electric Flow in a Circuit

In the previous chapter, the formulas for the calculation of a circuit's resistance levels were shared. However, the formulas for the *calculation of the entire load* in a circuit have yet to be discussed.

This is due to the significance of using the appropriate measurement units. In a few cases, especially those who are still on the initial phase of learning circuits? They aren't quite careful with their selected units. As it follows, it's not only necessary to calculate a circuit's electric flow; it's also necessary to calculate a circuit's flow correctly.

IV.A. – Standard Units

Among the several reasons to use *standard units of measurement* are for indications of exact measurements and for indications of the preferred measurements in a system. These units bring uniformity.

In circuits, the usual standard units that you encounter are *V, W, I,* and *P.* Although there are more, those who wish to explain a system's electric flow rely on these measurements; rather than introduce a bunch, which may only make matters more confusing, some are preferred. Moreover, without such units, understanding others' discussions of circuits is nearly impossible.

Standard units:

- Conductance – its measuring unit is Siemen with G as symbol

- Current – its measuring unit is ampere with I or i as symbol

- Frequency – its measuring unit is Hertz with Hz as symbol

- Inductance – its measuring unit is Henry with H or L as symbol

- Power – its measuring is watts with W as symbol

- Resistance – its measuring unit is ohm with R as symbol

- Voltage – its measuring unit is volt with V or E as symbol

IV.B. – Commonly Used Alternatives

Other than the *standard units of measurement*, other units are given light since these can enable clearer expression of the electric flow in a circuit. Especially if the circuit in subject contains a rather complex system, it can be difficult to arrive at a definite solution.

Other units:

- Angular frequency – it is a unit of measurement used in an AC circuit; it is a rotational unit that describes the relationship of at least 2 electric forms in a circuit

- Decibel – it is a unit of measurement that represent the gain in either current, power, or voltage; since it is only a tenth of the original unit, *Bel*, it is primarily reserved for denoting extremely small amounts

- Time constant – it is a unit of measurement that describes the output of a circuit's minimum or maximum output value; in a way, it refers to the measurement of time reaction

- Watt-hour – it is the unit of measurement that describes the electrical energy consumption over a period of time

IV.C. – Units of Force

Since *force* in a circuit is an important concept, it is advised that the particular unit of measurement is presented correctly. Even in physics, it is reiterated that it should be labeled according to its right category.

Atomic and electrostatic units of force:

- Hartrees

- Newtons

- Tesla

- Coulombs

- Meters

Chapter V – Power Transfer at Max

There will be instances of a *power transfer* in a circuit. For the electricity to continue its smooth flow, its original energy source will be replaced with an internal energy source. With such a change (especially in the case of a series circuit where power needs to flow continuously), the explanation for its system's pattern becomes a notch challenging.

For *beginners*, a great way of understanding *power transfer* in a circuit is to understand maximum power transfer, along with the concepts that dwell on the topic. As it follows, by gaining clarity on how much was the original power, as well as how much power a particular circuit can handle, you can see whether a power transfer is necessary or will only cause its load to be compromised.

V.A. – Maximum Power Transfer

Maximum power transfer, a concept that was introduced by Moritz von Jacobi sometime in the 1840s, draws light on the idea that for maximum external power to be obtained, an internal resistance needs to be in place. However, the transfer can only be flawless if the original resistance is equal to the potential power that an internal resistor can produce.

Consequently, maximum power transfer yields results that point out *power transfer*, and not *efficiency*; while improved efficiency can be a byproduct, it is not the chief purpose of maximum power transfer. It implies that although higher percentage of power is transferrable, it does not affect the magnitude of the power load (i.e. the extent that it can affect a circuit). In the event that the internal resistance is modified to accommodate a value higher than the value of the original resistance, improved efficiency can be achieved.

Moreover, the concept of maximum power transfer was initially misunderstood; a subject of many arguments was a circuit's reduced efficiency with the occurrence of transfer. Some insisted that due to the potential power that is lost during an exchange, a circuit may fail to reach 100% efficiency. As emphasis of this group's angle, take for example the case of a motor whose power is transferred from a battery; power in this situation may not be maximized, and it will only be realized over time when battery power has been fully consumed.

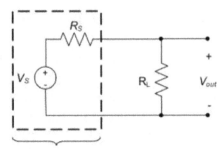

The maximum power theory states that the task of transferring power consumes power, too

It was *Thomas Edison*, as well as his fellow scientists, *Francis Robbins Upton*, who contested that maximum power transfer and efficiency are only *relative*; the 2 concepts are not one and the same. In fact, there is a discussion about *maximum power efficiency*, too.

In the exchange, you will find that *resistance* plays an important role. By giving light to the former argument, you can calculate a circuit's capability of a maximum power transfer, in relation to maximum power efficiency with the following formula:

MPT = RL ÷ (RL + RS)

A circuit's *MPT* (or maximum power transfer) can be determined with basic arithmetic skills. First, divide the *RL* (or Resistance Load) by the sum of the *RL* and *RS* (or Resistance Source).

V.B. – Thevenin's Theory

Thevenin's Theory, conceptualized by Hermann von Helmholtz and Leon Charles Thevenin, discusses that if a circuit follows a linear network, any point can be replaced given that it remains to carry a source for current, resistance, and voltage. Behind it, the idea is to supply an equivalent.

Originally, *Thevenin's Theory* can only be applied to circuits that operate with a DC system; since a DC system is rather simple, replacing its components with an equivalent is possible. Eventually, however, its capability to handle a load in a non-linear system was discovered; it can offer solutions for an AC system.

Moreover, the *Thevenin Theory* puts emphasis on that the average circuit can only be considered to have a linear according to a limited range; it can only be replaced by the components of with values among the range.

The Thevenin Theory follows that power dissipation can yield unique values, and can also yield identical values. However, the results can only be accomplished with the power supplied by an external resistor.

V.C. – The Star Delta Transformation

The *Star Delta Transformation* dwells on the idea that a circuit's system can change from one phase to another. For instance, if a circuit's power source is altered, its ability of carrying power from a point to the next is altered, too. Especially if there are 3 branches in a circuit's system, the power that circulates is known to form a closed loop.

The Star Delta Transformation refers to 2 kinds of circuit transformations. The first circuit transformation is a star transformation, which can be described by a "Y" formation; the second circuit transformation is a delta transformation, which can be described by a triangular pattern.

Moreover, the Star-Delta Transformation describes a 3-phase network of circuits, which can explain power transfer between these 3 networks. It enables the conversion of impedances that are connected to each other. With the theory as basis, alongside getting a clear scope for power transfer analysis, solving various concerns can be accomplished, too; the concept is applicable to different types of circuits including *series circuits, bridge-type networks, resistive circuits,* and *parallel circuits.*

The Star-Delta Transformation can be converted to the Delta-Star Transformation. From the star or Y-formation, the circuit creates a triangular network as the transition is achieved.

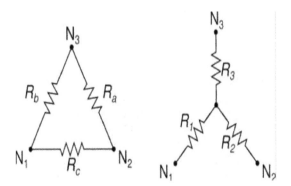

The Star-Delta Transformation or the Delta-Star Transformation is also called the Y-Δ Transformation or the Δ-Y Transformation

For the transition of the Star-Delta Transformation into the Delta-Star Transformation, a formula should be followed; this is meant to ensure that the transformation, along with the calculations for the total resistance in *all 3 circuits*, is successful. Initially, the goal is to compare the amount of power in an individual network. Once the power in network 1 has been acknowledged, proceed to identifying the weight that one network holds in the entire formation; one way of determining this is to disconnect that entire network and observe the operations of a circuit.

The formula:

**representations: $_\Delta R =$ total resistance of the transformation

$_1N =$ resistance in node 1

$_2N =$ resistance in node 2

$_AR =$ resistance in circuit A

$_BR =$ resistance in circuit B

$_CR =$ resistance in circuit C

$$_\Delta R \, (_1N \, _2N) = {}_CR \, || \, (_AR + {}_BR)$$

The simple version of the formula:

**representation: $_TR =$ total resistance

$_AR =$ resistance in circuit A

$_BR =$ resistance in circuit B

$_CR =$ resistance in circuit C

$$_TR = {}_AR + {}_BR + {}_CR$$

V.D. – Extra Element Theory

A circuit analysis technique that can be used for the simplification of a complicated problem is *the Extra Element Theory*; it was proposed by R.D. Middlebrook. The idea behind it is to take a complex matter, then divide it into small portions; each of the small portions will be addressed.

It follows that every circuit has a *transfer function* and *driving point*; the process of analyzing a circuit, therefore, can become easier if the aforementioned elements are first identified.

In the Extra Element Theory, unlike in other circuitry theorems, an element such as a capacitor or resistor can be temporarily removed so the transfer function or driving point can be determined. Since there are circuit components that can complicate an equation (regardless of how integral they are to a circuit), it is practical to set them aside for a while; although they may be of value to a circuit as a whole, it was proven that they don't affect calculations. Once the initial goal is achieved, the elements can be returned.

Impedance is a familiar term in discussions of the Extra Element Theory; it can be analyzed with the employment of the theory. In certain cases, its input can be determined in network granted that an *extra element* joins in.

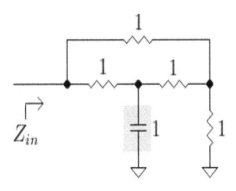

The Extra Element Theory (in relation to input impedance) proposes the addition of an "extra" element that is equivalent in value to the other elements

The formula for finding the impedance is:

**representations: Z = impedance

s = source

Z = 1 ÷ s

V.E. – Simplification of the Source

Simplification of the Source, sometimes referred to as Source Transformation, is the process of converting electric current into voltage, or voltage into electric current. It is a common technique used by many circuit engineers for explaining their circuit's system in simple terms.

The process of Simplification of the Source usually begins with an existing resistance source in a circuit; it is then replaced with new electric current source with a similar level of resistance. Since it is *bilateral procedure,* one can be derived to yield results from another. It makes way for the adjustment of voltage as it gradually becomes the equivalent of a particular circuit's resistance.

Moreover, *Simplification of the Source* may begin with an existing resistance, but is *not limited to the accommodation of resistive circuits.* It means that the process can be performed on circuits that involve inductors and capacitors.

V.F. – Where Does the Rosenstark Method Fit in?

The *Rosenstark Method,* sometimes called *Asymptotic Gain Model,* is yet another important subject where power transfer is concerned. In light of the return ratio, it serves as the representation of *negative gain* from feedback amplifiers. As it provides an intuitive form of circuit analysis, it introduces a new batch of elements such as the *return ratio* and *asymptotic gains.*

The Rosenstark formula:

**representations: G_o = 0 asymptotic gain

G_∞ = infinite asymptotic gain

T = return ratio

Rosenstark Method = $\{G_o + [T \div (T + 1)]\} + \{G_\infty + [T \div (T + 1)]\}$

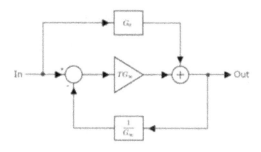

The Rosenstark Method serves as the basic representation of power transfer in a circuit

Best features of the Rosenstark Method:

- Assumes that the direct transmission is small and can be equated to the asymptotic gain

- Characterizes bilateral properties and feedback amplifiers

- Identifies (via thorough inspection) the passive circuit elements

Steps:

1. Choose a source in a circuit's system; preferably, opt for a dependent source.

2. Determine the source's return ratio.

3. Identify the G_∞.

4. Identify the G_0.

5. Use the Rosenstark formula and substitute values.

Chapter VI – Laws, Laws & More Laws

Come to think of it, *circuit analysis* is one of the broad branches of electrical engineering. It covers the basics of circuits and power consumption; it also covers the extensive aspects of the topic such as the operations of an entire electrical network.

Without laws regarding how electric current is distributed within a circuit's components, there is a risk of unclear discussions of *fundamental and in-depth analysis*; without them, a guide that can break down lengthy components is absent. For beginners, especially, they are important since they grant the chance to understand the functions of a circuit and even each one of its parts. It stays true to the idea that for the resolution of a big problem, looking at it like little pieces is an opportunity to conqueror its difficulties.

VI.A. – Putting Kirchhoff's Laws into Motion

Kirchhoff's Laws are composed of *2 equations* that dwell on the conservation of charge and energy. They were initially introduced in 1845 by Gustav Kirchhoff as a means for the determination of a circuit's power consumption, as well as its parameters.

As several discussions go, Kirchhoff's Laws may not be too important since it was derived from the work of Scottish physicist, *James Maxwell*; since it was derived from another's work, it is said that a circuit engineer should rather use the original work as basis. However, it is a set of laws that primarily focuses on the operations of a closed circuit; the previous work from which it was taken doesn't put emphasis on a closed circuit, and is rather descriptive of the generic circuit.

Moreover, Kirchoff's Laws are conditional. It may be useful in describing charge and energy conservation for different circuit elements, but it can only yield an *approximation*; it also requires certain factors such as changing electric currents, voltage, and resistance.

Kirchhoff's Law is actually a general term. To be specific, it addresses 2 subjects: current and voltage. It acknowledges all circuits, regardless of complexities.

To solidify its argument in the conservation of charge and energy, one of Kirchhoff's Laws, *KCL* (or Kirchhoff's Current Law), states that the electric current in an interconnected network is relative. And, to emphasize his point, Gustav Kirchhoff contests that the algebraic sum of the electric current in a joint network is *0*.

Another law of Kirchhoff that complements the KCL is *KVL* (or Kirchhoff's Voltage Law). Its basis is on the general law on energy conservation that defines voltage as the energy per unit of charge. Just like in the previous law, Gustav Kirchhoff says that in a closed network, the algebraic sum of the electric voltage in a joint network is *0*.

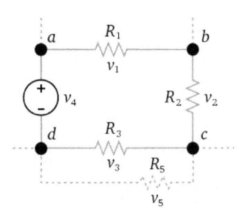

According to KVL, adding all the voltages within the circuit yields 0

VI.B. – Does Michael Faraday Know What He's Getting Into?

The *Law of Induction* by *Michael Faraday* is a fundamental law that revolves around the field of a circuit and the possible elements that are subject to eventual interaction. It carries both qualitative and quantitative aspects, and proposes that only with the presence of an infinite source of inductors can a circuit retain its inductive capability.

Unfortunately, not all circuit engineers and scientists are one with *Michael Faraday* and his *Law of Induction*. It is argued that although it holds some matters true, especially where loops of wire are concerned, it can yield the wrong results if used extensively; it can only handle a certain field and is usually arbitrarily small. In fact, counterexamples were previously presented.

A counterexample of Faraday's Law of Induction is the case involving an *electric disc generator*. Due to its own magnetic field, it can rotate circularly at a specified angular rate; it can complete a rotation and in the process, induct electricity by distributing it to other areas (within the circuit). It can be deduced that although the circuit's shape has remained constant over a period of time and although it can induct electricity, its distributive method made it lose inductive capabilities.

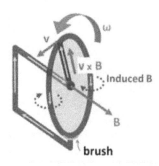

An electric disc generator induces electricity until cycle completion in the object's lower brush.

Faraday's Law of Induction may have been noted for certain flaws, but it is a law that made the conception of other important laws (not all of them are in the field of circuit engineering) possible. An important law with basis on Michael Faraday's idea is Albert Einstein's *Special Relativity*.

VI.C. - Ohm's Law & Conductivity

Ohm's Law, named after the German scientist, Georg Simon Ohm, is a powerful law that describes the resistance and electric current in a circuit, as well as their potential difference. Particularly, it sheds light on 2 points, then, subjects them to further analysis. Consequently, the relationship between Point A and Point B will indicate each of their properties as individual components.

In the verge of learning its concepts, it will dawn on you that *Ohm's Law* is an *empirical matter*. After observations with different ranges of length scales, it was proposed that it would fail where small wires are concerned; however, this proved to be a mere assumption since it was discovered that it could function regardless of a wire's size.

Since it is a basic equation in circuit engineering, *Ohm's Law* can also be applied for the determination of metal conductivity; it can be relied on when it comes to understanding the electric flow and conductive aspect in a circuit's component. Various materials that make use of Georg Ohm's principles are referred to as *ohmic*.

Georg Ohm set the parameters for his law to include only common terms in circuitry

In the physics of electricity, Ohm's Law is important where quantitative measurements in a circuit are concerned. Initially, when it was presented to German scientists, it was only mocked and rejected due to the mere fact that it went against the basic understanding of electric flow; it was dismissed as "a web of fancies" and worse, Georg Ohm was dubbed as a "fancy but invaluable" science professor. It was only until 1840 when it earned recognition and is now widely used today.

How to calculate for the elements in Ohm's Law:

Formula # 1:

voltage = current* resistance

Formula # 2:

current = voltage ÷ resistance

Formula # 3:

resistance = voltage ÷ current

VI.D. – The Argument of Norton's Theorem

Edward Lawry Norton, as he implies in *Norton's Theorem*, proposed that in circuit analysis, any linear network, granted that it has sources of voltage, electric current, and resistance, has an equivalent in dual network. A certain system may be unique, but values that can make a similar model can be obtained.

To find a circuit's equivalent using Norton's concepts, certain values need to be identified: voltage, electric current, and resistance. Once there are clear sources, you can begin formulating the necessary equations. However, when the sources are dependent on each other, another (and it has to be from a generic source) electric current needs to enter the picture.

Moreover, Norton's Theorem gives light to the fact that the values for the *equivalent current* and *equivalent voltage* are values that can be identified at the first 2 terminals of a circuit. It is important to note, however, that such a case is only possible if all the components in the said circuit are *short-circuited*. If the components are not short-circuited, a practical solution is to have current and voltage sources replaced; current can be replaced by transforming a circuit into an open circuit, and voltage can be replaced by transforming a circuit into a short circuit.

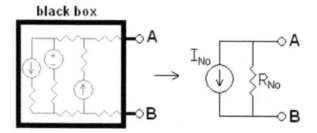

Norton's Theorem was also developed by Hands Ferdinand Mayer

The formula:

**representations: TC_{AB} = total current in circuit A and circuit B

TC = total current

TC_{AB} = voltage ÷ (TC in circuit A + TC in circuit B)

VI.E. – Coulomb's Law

One of the laws that underwent heavy testing is a law that gives importance to the electrostatic relationship of all the charged elements within a circuit; this law is called *Coulomb's Law* after the scientist, Charles Agustin de Coulomb. It argues that the magnitude of interactive circuit components is in direct proportion to the *squared area* between the distances. To demonstrate a point, it shows that the primary force works along a straight line.

Moreover, Coulomb's Law requires that the placement of the charged elements is accomplished through a single medium. This causes the arrangement to eliminate any possible complications.

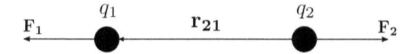

The application of Coulomb's Law is only valid if the circuit components are point charges

To make it effortless to obey Coulomb's Law, the determination of *Coulomb's constant* is recommended. Once the value of the constant has been determined, not only is it easier to adhere to the aforementioned law, you are also ensuring that the calculations for the electric current are valid.

The formula:

**representations: CC = Coulomb's Constant

ε_o = electric constant

$CC = 1 \div 4\pi \times \varepsilon_o$

Chapter VII – Understanding Electromagnetism

A pair of loudspeakers is an example of an electronic device that works due to the *strategic positioning* of circuit elements. That, along with the integral parts called *electromagnets*; such components cause disturbance to other circuit elements. Their effect on their fellows is rather significant as they tend to make the device's cone to vibrate. As a result, sound, and in most cases, high quality sound, is produced.

For a deeper understanding of a loudspeaker, you could use a lesson in *electromagnetism*.

VII.A. – An Introduction to the Concept behind Electromagnetism

Electromagnetism is a branch of science that involves the study of electricity and magnetism. It follows that wherever there is an electric field, there is also a magnetic field. It was initially introduced and developed by *Hans Christian Orsted*. In 1802, an Italian scholar by the name of *Gian Domenico Romagnosi* also examined the field

In circuitry, understanding the concept behind electromagnetism is important due the possibly strong electromagnetic reaction of circuit components. It follows that the *EMF* (or electromagnetic force) of any circuit serves a major role in the determination of internal properties.

Chapter V, *Power Transfer at Max*, and Chapter VI, *Laws, Laws & More Laws,* contain different discussions about transferring electric current and voltage. In electromagnetism, more discussions about transfer will be tackled. This time, however, the focus is on the charged elements in a circuit (whether negatively or positively charged), as well as their responses when exposed to movement.

The primary principles of electromagnetism:

- The direction of a magnetic field dictates the direction of the current in a circuit

- The electric current of a conductor creates a magnetic field; the formation is dependent on the direction of the conductor, but is always shaped in a corresponding circle

- The magnetic poles of charged elements always come in pairs; one pole in a pair needs to be inversely proportional to the other

- Charged elements can either attract or repel; elements with different charges are attractive to each other, while those with similar charges avoid contact

- Electric current can be induced when it is moved away or toward a magnetic field

VII.B. – Gauss Who?

A notable individual in the field of electromagnetism is *Carl Friedrich Gauss*. He is a German mathematician who put together the critical electromagnetism concepts in the form of a law called *Gauss Law*. According to him, to determine the relevance of the distribution of electric charges, the circuit's electric field, in its entirety, must be evaluated.

Gauss Law allows mathematical expression with the employment of *integral* and *differential calculus*, preferably in vector form. For a beginner in circuitry, the particular technique of demonstration is advised since it grants a clear perspective of the concept of electromagnetism.

The integral formula:

**representations: Φ_E = electric field

ε_0 = electric constant

Q = total electric charge

$$\Phi_E = Q \div \varepsilon_0$$

The differential formula:

**representations: ∇ = an electric field's divergence

E = the other half of an electric field's divergence

p = electric charge density

ε_0 = electric constant

$$\nabla \times E = p \div \varepsilon_0$$

VII.C. – The Main Formulas in Electromagnetism

In a circuit's electromagnetic field, it is important to remember that charged elements tend to move radically; sometimes, predicting the direction of the electric flow is nearly impossible. While others go about in a non-linear network, many charges obey the rule of superposition since they adhere to a linear path. With the use of certain laws as basis, the relationship between the charged elements can be evaluated.

4 laws:

37

1. Ampere's Law – an important law whose applications include instances of a moving magnetic field; particularly, it be applied in situations involving current-carrying wires

   The formula:

   **representations: B = electromagnetic field

   DL = differential element of the electric current

   μo = permeability of o space

   I = electric current in an enclosed circuit

   $\int B \times DL = \mu o \times I$

2. Biot-Savart's Law – a law that is employed for the calculation of steady current in an electromagnetic field; a requirement is a constant time variable, as well as a charge that is a subject of neither a build-up or depletion

   The formula:

   **representations: B = electromagnetic field outside a circuit

   μo = permeability of o space

   I = electric current in an enclosed circuit

   R = distance from the electromagnetic field

   $B = \int (\mu o \times I) \div 4\pi R^2$

3. Faraday's Law – like his [Michael Faraday] law of induction, this is a law that addresses the induced electromagnetic force of an object; it is strictly applicable to the charged elements within a closed circuit

   The formula:

   **representations: IEMF = induced electromagnetic field

   $D\varphi$ = difference of space

   DT = time differential

   $IEMF = - D\varphi \div DT$

4. Lorentz Force – a law that assesses a point charge due to both an electromagnetic field and an electric field

   The formula:

**representations: LF = Lorentz Force

q = total charge

EMF = electromagnetic field inside a circuit

V = velocity

B = electromagnetic field outside a circuit

$$LF = q \, [EMF + (V \times B)]$$

VII.D. – Electrodynamics & Quantum Electrodynamics

Before the 1900s, a scientist named William Gilbert addressed a proposal concerning *electricity* and *magnetism*; according to him, while both subjects can be traced to attracting and repulsing objects within a circuit, electricity and magnetism are different concepts. The key to understanding electromagnetism, therefore, is to understand the individual terms; particularly, understand their relevance and distinction.

A conflict regarding electromagnetism is that, despite agreeing to Albert Einstein's *Special Relativity*, it goes against some of the rules of mechanics; it is only dependent on the electromagnetic permeability of 0 space. It follows that in the case of moving frames, the electromagnetic field is subjected to transformation to include space.

Moreover, all electromagnetic phenomena are covered under *quantum mechanics*. This makes the electromagnetic field of a circuit accountable for the physical phenomena that are observable, especially *magnetism* and *electricity*.

Chapter VIII – Let's Talk Circuit Boards

Are you familiar with *crocodile clips*?

Crocodile clips are devices that can be used for the assembly of a circuit; these tools are so-named for their resemblance to the jaws of a crocodile. With them, a solid grip to connect a component is possible. If you're wondering how electrical engineers can create electrical connections without the associated dangers? Well, there's your answer.

By using *crocodile clips,* you can make a model of a working circuit. Whether be it a basic circuit, a series circuit, or a parallel circuit, you can create for an audience to analyze.

VIII.A. - Printed Circuit Boards 101

Printed circuit boards (or PCBs) are devices that enable electrical connectivity even in an "open" environment; within their system, there are resistors, inductors, transformers, capacitors, conductors, and semi-conductors. These tools support high component density. In a way, printed circuit boards are referred to as *live circuits.*

Since functioning circuit boards can be rather risky, especially when exposed to extreme environments, they are packaged accordingly. In most cases, these devices are subjected to a series of coating procedures and are dipped in acrylic, wax, polyurethane, and epoxy.

Design standards:

- Templates and card dimensions are designed according to required circuitry regulations

- Manufactured Gerber data are generated

- Design is planned thoroughly with the assistance of an *EDA or Electronic Design Automation* tool

- Traces for signals are routed

- Copper thickness and layer thickness are carefully evaluated

VIII.B. – Circuit Board Tests

To see if a circuit works, certain tests are performed. Particularly, it is determined whether or not it is functional and can perform desired tasks. Along with its capacitors, resistors, transformers, and other components, it is analyzed for opens and shorts.

Objectives of testing methods:

- To detect flaws

- To detect error-free operations of each of its components

- To determine system stability

- To evaluate whether it is fit for use

- To evaluate safety issues

- To verify test systems

Example testing methods:

- Analog tests

- Contact tests

- Contact tests

- Electrolytic capacitor tests

- Flash tests

- Powered digital tests

- Short tests

VIII.C. – Let's Learn to Prototype

Prototyping is the ability to put a particular idea to test by preparing a model from which other circuits are developed. Especially when the circuit in subject involves a complex system or expensive components, a prototype is initially designed.

If the circuit creator is unsure of how a particular circuit will function, his best bet is to create a *prototype*. This way, he can evaluate his creation and see how it can be improved. If it's not yielding his desired results, he can modify the placements of each of its components until he achieves a necessary output. Otherwise, he can proceed to the actual circuit-making process.

VIII.D. - The Art of Bread-Boarding

Breadboards allow the creation of a circuit prototype, which is the reason why these tools are ideal for beginners. *Bread-boarding*, therefore, is the process of creating a circuit prototype in a board to resemble the operations of a real circuit. Its history can be traced to the time that electrical enthusiasts would use a literal breadboard (i.e. the board used for slicing bread).

According to experts, it's recommended to learn and understand bread-boarding prior to making your first-ever circuit. It's advised to be familiar with each of its components, as well as how it works.

Breadboard components:

- Chips – these are *legs* that come out of both sides of a breadboards; these components fit perfectly and serve as connectors of different parts

- Posts – these are components that enable connections from power sources

- Power rails – these are vertical metal rows strips that are adjacent to terminals; through these components, easy access to a power source can be provided

- Power supplies – these are components that enable the supplementation of a wide range of electric current and voltage levels

- Terminals – these are horizontal metal row strips that are adjacent to power rails; through these components, wires are allowed to be inserted, then, be held intact

VIII.E. – Essential Skills in Circuitry

After understanding *bread-boarding*, you're almost ready for some hands-on circuit lessons. First, however, you should adopt a certain set of skills; while bread-boarding is helpful, it's only practice (i.e. for instance, there is no soldering involved). Since you'll be making an actual functioning circuit, it's time to get your hands dirty.

5 skills required in circuitry:

1. Stripping (wire) – it is a skill that promotes secure electrical connections; it involves the knowledge on various types of wires, thickness of wires, and how to maintain a solid grip; since exposure to electric current is a risk, it is best to check out the appropriate tools for wires

2. Drilling – it is a skill that focuses on the proper drilling (of holes) in a circuit, then, making sure that electrical connections can remain intact; it is a slow process that requires practice with accuracy and precision

3. How to test batteries – it is a skill that requires testing the capacity of a battery; particularly, it involves measuring the current load in open and short circuits

4. How to use a glue gun – it is a skill that takes advantage of a glue gun's conductive property; it teaches how to insulate and how to set a semi-permanent coating; especially when there is a need to strengthen the joints of a circuit, it comes in handy

5. How to use liquid electrical coating – it is a skill that focuses on the ability to apply liquid electrical coating where conventional electrical tape is likely to fail; it requires precaution since about 30% of the parts in the liquid coating are quite volatile

VIII.F. – The Secrets of a Solder

Soldering is a process that involves (at least) 2 metals (or any conductive material); the 2 metals are joined by flowing and melting. In the industry of circuitry, it is one of the most fundamental methods in circuit creation; it allows independent components to work as one.

A technique of good soldering revolves around the knowledge of the amount of heat that is applied. For *basic soldering, 361F* is the temperature to consider and for *advanced soldering*, the goal is to arrive at a temperature of somewhere between *361F to 419F.*

In *metallurgical engineering*, a term named *flux* is commonly used; in circuit engineering, as soon as the circuit creation process commences, it will be introduced, too. It is cleaning agent and a flowing material that facilitates the soldering process. Should there be invisible impurities (e.g. oil, dirt, etc.), they will be removed for the purpose of not risking the integrity of a circuit.

Moreover, it is important to note that in soldering, the proper application of flux is suggested. Improper methods can result to joint failure. The system's damage (due to incorrect flux application) may not be obvious at first, but gradually, it is capable of corrosion and rendering a circuit useless.

Chapter IX – Sufficient Safety

On a sunny day, try heading outside of your house, then, checking out the electrical connections (wires) from one post to another. More likely, one, two, or even a flock of birds are calmly resting on power lines.

Do you ever wonder why they don't get shocked?

No, birds are normal creatures; they do not possess extra-special powers. In their heads, they understand that it's a must not to step on open electrical networks, which is one of the things that need to be covered for beginners in circuit engineering.

IX.A. – The Lack of Electrical Safety Courses

While some *circuit engineering professors* teach enough lessons about *electrical safety*, others are quite behind on the area. They assume that practical knowledge, as well as a general "be careful" would suffice; since the beginners in circuit engineering are frequent exposure to electrical devices, no, the statement won't cut it. Therefore, it is important to stress out the need to be careful especially during their first hands-on activity.

Electrical safety tips:

- Treat each electrical device as if live current is running inside it (regardless if you're aware that there isn't)

- Overloading sockets for a circuit board? Not a good idea

- To cut off running current, add a residual current

- Always disconnect (and not just turn off) electrical devices when working on a component

- Always turn off any electrical device if not in use

- Regularly check the conditions of sockets and plugs

- Practice extreme caution when dealing with liquids and electric current

- Make sure your hands are dry

- Avoid octopus connections (i.e. devices that enable multiple plugs or sockets)

- Keep electrical wires and cords tucked neatly

- Wear the proper attire when creating a circuit; put on non-conductive gloves and footwear with insulated soles

IX.B. - The Importance of Hands-on Circuit Lessons

Hands-on learning is important for a beginner in circuits. It gives light to the fact that in circuit engineering, it is more about actual field work. Once the concepts are understood, it's best to move on to creating functional circuit boards.

A common problem that is encountered by beginners? Sweaty hands. Even in an air-conditioned laboratory, there are people who have to deal with sweaty hands when handling circuits. Alongside, they have to deal with the need of maintaining a strong and solid grip on various tools. Although this may be a concern, it's one that requires practice.

IX.C. – The 80-20 Rule of Circuit Safety

In circuitry, there is a rule that focuses on the installments of transmitters in hazardous areas for devices with a circuit; it is called the *80-20 Rule of Circuit Safety*. According to the rule, it is recommended to take extra precaution when dealing with particular portions of an electronic device; there are some parts that increase the risk of electrical shock when *touched* or *moved*.

Hazardous areas of a circuit (that require extra precaution):

- Point with high impedance

- Point with high resistance

- Area near the voltage source

- Area near an opening

- Area with conductive elements

IX.D. – Troubleshooting Concerns

In the event that a device with a circuit is not function correctly, it is recommended to have it evaluated accordingly. While a beginner may handle the task of checking, a professional in circuitry is the one who is advised to assess the system. Since an expert is already familiar with different circuit components, and he knows exactly where to look for possible faults, he is more qualified for the job.

Troubleshooting tips:

- Determine whether the connections are secure

- Determine whether the wires are correctly connected to one another

- Check for circuit components that seem out of place

- Check for circuit components that may be larger in size

Chapter X – Here's a Multimeter for You!

An important and indispensible tool in circuitry is a *multimeter*.

Imagine a situation when a circuit project was presented to you. Since you were requested to detail accurate measurements for its electric current, voltage, and resistance, you go to the nearest equipment laboratory to borrow a stack of devices for assistance.

Now, imagine the same situation, but this time, you have this tool; instead of having to go to the equipment laboratory to borrow a stack of devices to measure the electric current, voltage, and resistance, you turn to that tool. This particular time, you have a multimeter.

If you're not familiar with the operations of a multimeter, let it be your first job prior to creating a circuit project. It's actually quite easy to use. So long as you are attentive to instructions, and you know its components, certain restriction, and the technique to maximizing its functions, you're set.

X.A. - What's a Multimeter?

A multimeter, also called a multitester, *Volt-Ohm millimeter*, and *Volt-Ohm meter*, is an electronic device that measures the electric current in a circuit; it is capable of measuring voltage, resistance, and a variety of other units in a circuit's system. To know how to use the device, it's important to be familiar with each of its components; if you can understand how the components work, you can also understand the operations of the entire device.

Parts of a multimeter:

1. The selection knob – it enables a user to choose a particular setting that is subject for measurement

2. The display meter – it enables the display of the measured reading; it can contain up to 4 digits, as well as a negative sign

3. The probes – these are plugged into a multimeter that can interpret and convert measurements from a device into a multimeter; usually, these come in a pair of red and black probes

   Types of probes:

   I.   IC hook

   II. Alligator clips

   III. Test probes

X.B. - A Multimeter in the Works

Inarguably, a multimeter is one of the most useful tools in circuitry and one of the tools that can make the task of building circuits easy. It can be used to measure *any object or device* that contains a circuit and an electric current. Using it, however, comes the hard part; in fact, in the world of circuits and electronics, it earned the title as one of the most challenging jobs. It may be effortless to get a reading, but getting an accurate reading, then interpreting the reading is another story.

How to use a multimeter to measure (a basic example):

1. Prepare an AAA battery.

2. Plug the black probe of a multimeter to the negative side (i.e. the side with a "-") of the AAA battery.

3. Plug the red probe of a multimeter to the positive side of the AAA battery.

4. Check the display meter; as recommended, check the meter twice.

5. List down the reading and begin the interpretation.

X.C. – Resolution, Accuracy & Input Impedance

The smallest part of a multimeter's scale is called as the *resolution*. It is responsible for achieving an accurate reading and interpretation. In many multimeter kinds, especially digital ones, it can be configured or *calibrated*. And, as the rules go, a device with low resolution doesn't require much completion time; a device with high resolution can require a demanding processing time.

Meanwhile, the *accuracy* of a multimeter refers to an error in the measurement of an electric current, in comparison to a perfect reading. It is relative to the device's resolution since resolution may not be calibrated accordingly if the absolute accuracy level is questionable. Therefore, to determine the total accuracy of a multimeter, its relative accuracy should be added to its absolute accuracy.

Formula for the computation of total accuracy:

**representations: TA = total accuracy

RA = relative accuracy

AA = absolute accuracy

$TA = RA + AA$

When talking about a multimeter's resolution and accuracy, *input impedance* is a set of terms that needs to be acknowledged, too. This is due to the device's inability to achieve accurate readings when it is not set accordingly. Especially for the measurement of a circuit's voltage, its input impedance has to be calibrated high (i.e. higher than a circuit's voltage) so the operation remains smoothly.

X.D. – Safety Concerns

Groups that are in charge of the manufacture of multimeters, as well as the authorities that promote the safe use of such devices have set safety standards. This is to emphasize the importance of the right employment of the electrical tools. Although the method for use can be rather straightforward, reckless habits can result to problems. Alongside the possibility of inaccurate readings, it can cause harm to the individual that is handling the devices.

Categories of safety standards:

- Category 1 – applicable to the employment of a multimeter, circuit, or any electronic equipment with a distance near main connections

- Category 2 – applicable to the employment of a multimeter, circuit, or any electronic equipment with a distance somewhere near the first phase of main connections

- Category 3 –applicable to the employment of a multimeter, circuit, or any electronic equipment with a distance near permanently installed loads

- Category 4 – applicable to the employment of a multimeter, circuit, or any electronic equipment with a distance near faulty current levels that can be quite high

Chapter XI - DIY Circuits: Simple Projects

When you're into circuits, as well as *electronics and electrical engineering*, you need to step up your game when it comes to building items. Isn't the main reason for learning the branch of electrical engineering for the creation of circuits, then, putting them to good use?

In the event that your first circuit project wouldn't turn out as desired, try not to get discouraged easily, and instead, give matters another go. Not getting the results you wanted maybe a bit of a downer, but eventually, the odds will be in your favor; look at the setback as an opportunity for learning. If your heart's into circuits, you'll soon get the hang of how things are done.

XI.A. – Common Tools in Circuitry

For the creation of a circuit, you can make use of just about any tool you come across; if you find equipment that will make you accomplish a task easier, then, maybe you should put it in your arsenal. You *can* use just any tool, yes, but, doing so is not advised. It is best to choose the right set (i.e. a set of tools with a non-conductive handle) to not put your safety at risk.

Common tools:

- Crimper

- Cutters (e.g. cable cutter, electrical cutter, etc.)

- Extraction tool

- Glue gun

- Non-metallic tweezers

- Pliers

- Screwdriver

- Soldering gun

- Wire-wrapping tools

XI.B. - Beginner Circuit Projects

Building your first circuit can be a challenge; since you're still a beginner, you may end up making mistakes. Maybe your circuit won't end up as functional as desired, despite having followed your understanding of a series of procedures. In such a case, this is where you have to tweak your work; be diligent in figuring out where you went wrong. If you're uncertain of your actions' impact, don't worry too much. The important part is to begin; you can, then, figure out the rest along the way.

7 easy circuit projects (derived from http://www.instructables.com):

- Project # 1 – Static Electricity Analyzer

    The Static Electricity Analyzer can detect nearby static electricity; to indicate that static electricity is present, its LED component glows. Apart from a detector, it can be used to analyze the electricity in its surroundings. It is an extremely sensitive device since it can even detect nearby hand movement without touching the antenna.

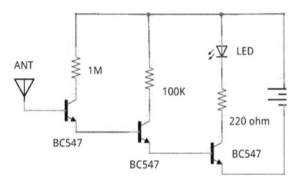

Materials:

- Around 10 pieces wire

- 1 piece LED

- 1 piece static electricity antenna

- 1 piece 100K resistor

- 1 piece 1M resistor

- 3 pieces 2n222 transistor

Procedures (as shown in the layout above):

1. To the left side of the circuit board, connect the 1M resistor to 2n222 transistor.

2. Beside it, attach the wire, then, attach the static electricity antenna.

3. On the bottom, attach the wire, then, attach the other 2n222 transistor; next to it, attach the wire, and finally, attach the third 2n222 transistor.

4. Place the 100K resistor adjacent to the second 2n222 transistor.

5. Place the LED adjacent to the third 2n222 resistor.

6. Establish connection to a power supply.

- Project # 2 – Dark LED Light

The Dark LED Light is a circuit project that can detect darkness. It follows that when insufficient light is supplied, an IC timer is alerted; consequently, a high output is produced and LED light will be switched on. The idea behind it is similar to that of a street light that automatically turns on once it detects that it's already evening.

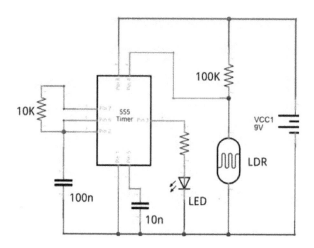

Materials:

- Around 10 pieces wire

- 1 piece LED

- 1 piece LDR

- 1 piece 10nf capacitor

- 1 piece 100nf capacitor

- 1 piece 10K resistor

- 1 piece 100K resistor

- 1 piece 555 IC timer

Procedures (as shown in the layout above):

1. On top of the LDR, attach the 100K resistor.

2. On the bottom of the LDR, create a connection to the LED.

3. To the left of the LED, create a connection to the 10nf capacitor.

4. To the left of the 10nf capacitor, create a connection to the 100nf capacitor.

5. Next to the 100nf capacitor, create a connection to the 10K resistor.

6. Place the 555 IC timer between all the connections; establish the main connection by attaching the other ends of the LED, LDR, capacitors, and resistors to the 555 IC timer (directly or with a wire).

7. Establish connection to a power supply.

- Project # 3 – The Ticking Bomb

The Ticking Bomb is meant for creating a ticking sound that resembles a bomb. Once it is turned on, it produces sound that is adjustable, but is modified to 1 tick per second.

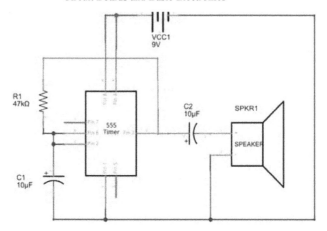

Materials:

- Around 10 pieces wire

- 2 pieces 10uf capacitors

- 1 piece 555 IC timer

- 1 piece 47K resistor

- 1 piece 8 ohm speaker

Procedures (as shown in the layout above):

1. Make the 555 IC timer as the central component; to its left, create a connection to the 47K resistor.

2. On the bottom, create a connection to the first 10uf capacitor; then, create a connection from the 10uf capacitor to the 47K resistor.

3. To the right of the 555 IC timer, create a connection to the second 10uf capacitor.

4. From the second 10uf capacitor, create a connection to the 8 ohm speaker.

5. Establish connection to a power supply.

- Project # 4 – The Remote Tester

The Remote Tester, as its name suggests, is a circuit that checks whether or not a remote control is working. Behind it, the idea is focused on the sufficient amount of signals that the IR receiver is getting. If it receives enough signals, the LED lights up, which means that a particular remote control is functioning; conversely, if the LED remains as is, it is an indication of a faulty component in the device.

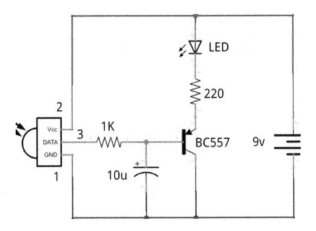

Materials:

- Around 10 pieces wire

- 1 piece LED

- 1 piece IR receiver

- 1 piece 1K resistor

- 1 piece bc557 transistor

- 1 piece 10uf capacitor

Procedures (as shown in the layout above):

1. On top of the bc557 transistor, create a connection to the LED.

2. Adjacent of the bc557 transistor (to the left), create a direct path to the 1K resistor, then, to the IR receiver.

3. On the bottom, create a connection to the 10uf capacitor.

4. Connect the 10uf capacitor (directly or with wire) to close the connection.

5. Establish connection to a power supply.

- Project # 5 – The Bell Experiment

The Bell Experiment is a basic project that produces a musical sound; the result is a device that may be similar to a doorbell. It works according to each of its components; if the resistor, transistor, and IC are triggered, the bunch sends a signal to the speaker, which will then, create the sound.

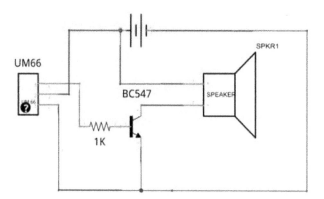

Materials:

- Around 10 pieces wire

- 1 piece 1K resistor

- 1 piece 2n222 transistor

- 1 piece UM66 IC

- 1 piece 8 ohm speaker

Procedures (as shown in the layout above):

1. On one end of the 8 ohm speaker, create a connection to the 2n222 transistor.

2. On another end, create a connection to the 1K resistor.

3. From the 1K resistor, create a connection to the UM66 IC; make sure that the UM66 is parallel to the 8 ohm speaker.

4. Connect the UM66 (directly or with wire) to the 2n222 transistor to close the circuit.

5. Establish connection to a power supply.

- Project # 6 – The LED That Fades

The LED That Fades is a project that produces and sometimes, blinking lights. It operates according to the weakness or strength of the signals that are interpreted by each of its components. If its IC timer, transistor, resistor, and capacitor receive strong signals; the LED will glow; conversely, if they receive weak signals, the light starts to fade. In the event that the signals that are submitted are unstable (i.e. they alternate between weak or strong in a few minutes' time), the blinking pattern comes in.

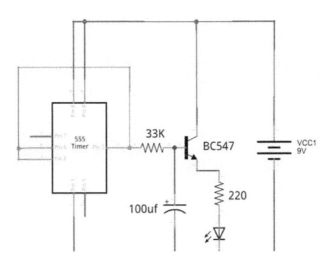

Materials:

- Around 10 pieces wire
- 1 piece LED
- 1 piece 555 IC timer
- 1 piece bc547 transistor
- 1 piece 33K resistor
- 1 piece 220 ohm resistor
- 1 piece 100uf capacitor

Procedures (as shown in the layout above):

1. To the bottom of the bc547 transistor, create a connection to the LED.
2. Parallel to the LED, create a connection to the 100uf capacitor.
3. On top of the 100uf 33K resistor, create a connection to the 220 ohm resistor.
4. Next to the 220 ohm resistor, create a connection to the 555 IC timer.
5. Create a connection around the 555 IC timer for a closed circuit.
6. Establish connection to a power supply.

- Project # 7 – The LED with Activated Light

The LED with Activated Light is a basic project for beginners in circuit engineering; it is meant for a clearer understanding of the concept of resistance. The LED lights up with the application of sufficient resistance; if resistance levels are insufficient, the light won't be activated.

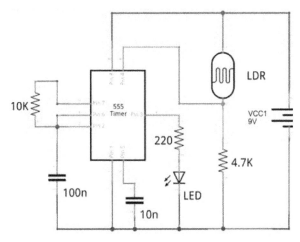

Materials:

- Around 10 pieces wire

- 1 piece LED

- 1 piece LDR

- 1 piece 10nf capacitor

- 1 piece 100nf capacitor

- 1 piece 10K resistor

- 1 piece 4.7K resistor

- 1 piece 555 IC timer

- 1 piece 220 ohm resistor

Procedures (as shown in the layout above):

1. To the bottom of the LDR, create a connection to the 4.7K resistor.

2. Parallel to the 4.7K resistor connection, create a new connection to the LED, followed by the 22 ohm resistor on top.

3. From the 22 ohm resistor, create a connection to the 555 IC timer.

59

4. To the bottom of the 555 IC timer, and parallel to the LED connection, create a new connection to the 10nf capacitor.

5. To the left of the 10nf capacitor, create a connection to the 100nf capacitor.

6. On top of the 100nf capacitor, create a connection to the 10K resistor.

7. Create a connection to close the circuit.

8. Establish connection to a power supply.

Chapter XII – Making Your Way to Circuit Design: PCB Layouts & Schematic Diagrams

If you are familiar with each of its components, you may have a good grasp of how an electronic circuit works; granted that the integral parts (e.g. power source, conductor, resistor, diode, etc.) are in place, and you were introduced to different techniques on establishing connections properly, there's a high chance that any circuit project you take on can be a success. Once an opening for a power source is identified, and the stability of an arrangement for the rest in a series is achieved, you're set.

However, if given the opportunity to make a particular circuit more functional, wouldn't you take it? Instead of settling for a random circuit design, why not have it modified for superior performance?

XII.A. - Circuit Design 101

Ever wonder why circuit engineers are paid highly and (depending on their chosen career path) are presented different career advancement opportunities (e.g. work as computer engineers, robotics specialists jobs, etc.)?

The responsibilities of circuit engineers are rather demanding; they need to be mentally tough and be open to different challenges. They spend hours and hours racking their brains out to determine how systems can be made more efficient. Chances are, there's always a way; it's up to them to look for one. When a particular project asks for it, it's mandatory for them to let their creative juices flow to arrive at a compatible solution. Otherwise, their built circuits may stop functioning eventually.

As mentioned, it's practical to design a circuit accordingly; especially with their employment for the fields of *communication, navigation, telecommunication, travel*, and other industries, their designs should consider a particular purpose. Apart from the objective of meeting different requirements, there needs to be a strategy since a more functional circuit comes with higher quality; it can make a project consume a reduced number of resources, too.

Reasons why there are various circuit designs:

- Improvement of a circuit's efficiency

- Improvement of a circuit's size and weight

- Guarantee a circuit's durability for a set period

- Guarantee a circuit is safe to use

XII.B. – The Design Process

Many times, a PCB layout (as discussed in chapter VII, *Let's Talk about Circuit Boards*) and a schematic diagram are often interchanged in circuitry; it has led others, especially the novices in circuit engineering, to believe that they are one and the same. In a way, since they are both presentations of a circuit's system, they may seem similar. However, upon closer inspection, they are not. It is, therefore, essential in the circuit design process that the difference is acknowledged.

A *PCB layout* is a physical representation or a *real model* of a circuit. It presents all of the electrical components that are included; it also details which of the components are active and which ones are passive. Although it can show an actual working circuit, understanding the functions of each of its parts can be tedious.

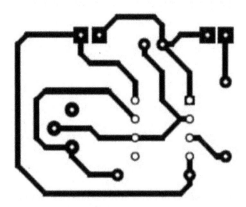

A PCB layout is an actual circuit model

On the other hand, a *schematic diagram*, also called simply as a circuit diagram, is a descriptive outline of a circuit's system; it is the standard and less costly way of circuit representation. It is like a PCB layout that shows both of the active and passive components in a circuit; unlike a PCB layout, however, its presentations can be easily understood.

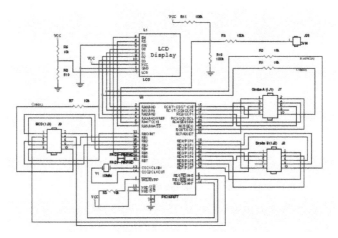

A schematic diagram can include important notes for the improvement of a circuit's design

Stages of circuit design:

- Meeting specific requirements

- The creation of a circuit diagram

- Building a breadboard, or a PCB layout

- The presentation of each circuit component (for professional evaluation)

- Applying the results of evaluation

- Testing (and retesting)

- Getting approval from professionals

Circuit design tips for beginners (preparation process):

- Categorize the components

- Construct a PCB layout, as well as a schematic diagram

- Determine the compatibility of each circuit component

Circuit design tips for beginners (circuit-building process):

- Always avoid cold solder joints

- Always separate power controls and other connections

- Always separate analog and digital components

- Create traces should hard-to-find components be included

- Remember to always make integral nodes accessible

- Solder the components systematically; solder small components first, then, solder larger components next

- Strategize the spaces you allow between components

- Take note of any heat spots

XII.C. - Circuit Symbols

On the process of building a circuit and modifying its design, an understanding of different circuit symbols is important. Descriptions of circuit components can be put in simple words; it is called a *verbal description*. However, since a thorough approach is recommended in many circuitry lessons, a visual representation can enable you to understand the electric flow in a circuit.

Here's a good comparison:

Verbal description	Visual representation
Circuit # 1 contains a light bulb, as well as D-cell battery as power source.	

Moreover, circuit symbols for a visual representation of a circuit is preferred over a verbal descriptions since they may be less complicated to understand. Especially if the particular circuit is quite advanced, a description containing words can be challenging to use as basis. If a visual model is employed, however, you can simply focus on connections, instead of the interpretation of a worded description; there is a better chance of building an impressive circuit design successfully. Especially if you have plans of advancing your place in circuit engineering by soon moving forward from a novice to a circuit expert, *memorizing* the different circuit symbols is a must.

List of basic symbols:

Symbol name	Symbol
AC	
DC	
Capacitor	
Resistor	
Fuse	
Diode	
LED	
Regulator	
Transistor	

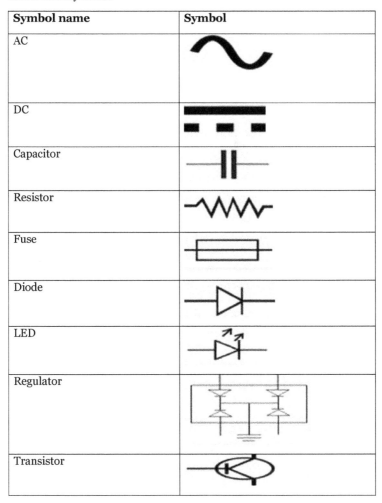

List of basic capacitor variation symbols:

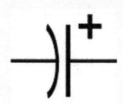

-

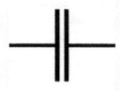

-

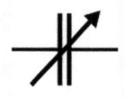

-

List of basic diode variation symbols:

-

Anode ⊳◁ Cathode

-

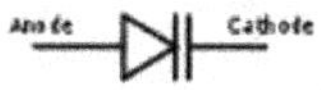

Anode ⊳|⊢ Cathode

-

Anode ⊳| Cathode

-

List of basic switches variation symbols:

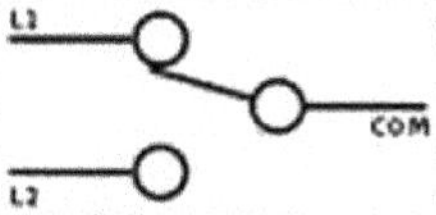

L1 ──○
        ○── COM
L2 ──○

-

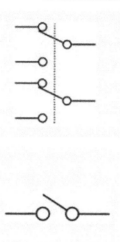

•

•

List of basic transistor variation symbols:

•

•

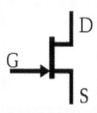

-

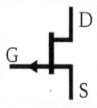

-

XII.D. – Factors to Consider

A strategic circuit design is important since a circuit may not function at all in the absence of a good plan; if the placement of each of its components wasn't accomplished according, you may have just wasted resources. You may have the correct components but if they are not designed properly, a circuit is far from working. Besides, at the realization that you may not be design a circuit's system according to requirements, you wouldn't want to put the circuit-building project to an end at the middle of the process, right?

Moreover, the proper design structure of a circuit needs to be prioritized. Regardless if it is not meant to impress another, it should still be designed accordingly as to be a stepping stone in the possibility of handling more projects eventually. With the knowledge of how to design a circuit properly as a beginner comes the effortless knowledge on the construction of more advanced circuits eventually.

What to keep in mind:

- Time availability (of the creator) – although it can be completed quickly, a circuit project shouldn't be rushed; the project creator should be available for a set period so he can concentrate properly on a circuit. Especially if he has hardly any time to spare, it's suggested that he either determines a way to find additional time, or takes on a different project

- Difficulty level – the assessment of a circuit project is important prior to acceptance. While there are simple ones, some projects are rather complicated. If a creator is certain that he can't follow through the procedures of a particular project, he may want to consider other undertakings

- Total cost of the project – one reason that the creation of a schematic diagram and other preparations are suggested (prior to taking on a circuit project) is due to practicality regarding the overall expenses. As much as possible, the creator should consider his ability to fund a project. Especially if he plans on using expensive circuit components, he needs to think about whether he can afford the project until completion.

- The desired function – identify the reason why you took on the project. Is it for experimentation and personal use? Or, was it a request from a company? Especially if the purpose is for a commercial company, design a circuit to achieve first-rate quality.

XII.E. - Documentation, Verification & Testing

A primary benefit of the *documentation* process is its advantage of letting you identify possible errors in putting together a circuit. If you weren't successful at the end stage of your project, you can figure out exactly where you went wrong; in favor of having to disregard your current progress and starting from scratch the second time around, you can simply have certain methods modified (for improvement).

Verification, as defined in circuitry, is the process of thoroughly evaluating each of a circuit's components, as well as each of the stages in the making. The objective is to determine whether the process has been adhered to correctly. Usually, this can be a time-consuming process, but since it is intend to ensure quality, it is an important one.

In a way, the real-world version of the verification process is *testing*. Prior to a circuit's launch and its exposure to different commercial industries, it is tested in research laboratories. Like verification, it can also be a time-consuming process, and since it is the last process before a circuit is passed on to another source, it can be a labor-intensive series.

Chapter XIII – A Way Is through EDA

Are you familiar with *FABS* or *Semi-conductor fabrication facilities?*

FABS are places where circuit designs, even complex ones, can be put together; they are usually extensive since they are meant to accommodate bulk circuit projects. Inside them are various equipment for *EDA*, which is why circuit-production is rapid.

With the productivity level of FABS, semi-conductors are continuously becoming popular. And, since semi-conductors are components in a circuit, circuits grew in popularity, too.

XIII.A. - What Is EDA?

EDA, also known as *Electronic Design Automation* is a class of software equipment especially for designing a circuit or different electronic devices. It is categorized along with other modern tools used in circuitry; it eliminates the need to design a circuit by hand, which minimizes simple and critical errors, repair glitches, and suggest possible improvements.

Moreover, it's due to EDA that circuit creation and circuit production became faster. If you're concerned regarding the quality since the process is done in an automated fashion, be confident that each design underwent thorough analysis. Remember, the software equipment's design was specifically meant to address a circuit's system.

XIII.B. – Design Flows

In the world of circuitry, it's important to be informed of the concepts of EDA; it privileges a circuit creator with a good grasp of the proper way to build circuits. The employees of grand electronics companies such as *Intel, Hewlett Packard*, and *Valid Logic Systems* are all trained to have impressive knowledge of the tools, despite already having gone through years of education.

Through the years, EDA tools have undergone continuous development. Initially, the concepts were rather limited; in the *Age of EDA Invention,* the focus was merely on *routing, logic synthesis, static analysis,* and *placement.* Eventually, in the *Age of EDA Implementation,* these concepts were subjected to major improvements; more *sophisticated and advanced algorithm* for the EDA tools were considered. Come the *Age of EDA Integration*, they were further studied and were designed to cater to integrated environments.

Now, you may be wondering why there is a need to build circuits manually when there are EDA tools. Well, although the process can be accomplished easier and faster, sometimes, bringing the expertise of a circuit engineer on the table is recommended; this way, he can thoroughly evaluate the quality of a circuit's system.

Additionally, the operators of EDA tools are selected carefully; usually, they are the ones with a background in the operations of EDA tools and similar equipment. This is due to the expenses, as well as the possible complications, involved in using such devices. In the event that a need for troubleshooting arises, it's best to have somebody who is knowledgeable in circuit designs on standby.

Primary focuses of EDA:

- The presentation of schematic-driven layout

- Advanced and logical interpretation of each circuit component

- Hardware and transistor simulation

XIII.C. - Circuit-Level Optimization

The circuit-level optimization or *power optimization* of EDA tools refers to the various techniques that are employed for the reduction of the total power in a circuit. Although the intent is to modify a circuit's setup economically, the processes shouldn't compromise the product's overall quality. With the main goal of enhancing a circuit's efficiency, the other objectives are to increase speed, eliminate possible leakage, enhance power distribution, and improve functionality.

Circuit-level optimization techniques:

- Modification of voltage scales, thresholds, variables, blocks, supplies, and other voltage-related concerns

- Modification and re-sizing of transistors

- Modification of logic styles

- Re-routing of networks

XIII.D. - Interpretation, Analysis & Verification

Although the automation process of EDA tools may eliminate errors in a circuit's system, a product remains a subject of various testing methods. This is due to the industry of circuitry's insistence on guaranteeing the flawless networks of circuit systems. In the aim of making sure that a circuit's functions are in tune with specific requirements, it is interpreted, analyzed, and verified.

In the event when a circuit (that was created with EDA tools) hadn't undergone tests, there is a likelihood that it won't function for a specific purpose. Especially if the project will be employed for commercial agenda, the industry experts are not granting permission to distribute "unevaluated" circuit systems.

Circuit evaluation methods:

- Assessment of a circuit's maintenance requirements
- Inspection of desired and undesired effects (in relation to mathematical logic)
- Inspection of a circuit's functionality
- Inspection of a circuit's stability
- Verification of physical components
- Verification of static timing

Chapter XIV – The Other Way around: Reverse Engineering

One of the coolest ways of understanding circuits is to disassemble all of its components one by one. First, make sure that it is not connected to any power source. After putting on protective gloves, begin taking apart a component; then, determine its function. Repeat the procedures until you know the purpose of the parts and the importance of having them work as a network.

Now, put them all back together; make sure the circuit works.

Such a process is called *reverse engineering*.

XIV.A. - An Introduction to Reverse Engineering

Reverse engineering, also called *deconstruction, reversing, backwards engineering,* and *back engineering* is the process of extracting knowledge from any device or electronic equipment. It involves the need to deconstruct an entire circuit for further analysis of its components. Although the methods that will be employed are opposite to the process of creation, it is considered as a practical approach of learning circuitry.

Moreover, reverse engineering gives light to Aristotle's concept that the key to understanding the operations of a device is studying each one of its parts. Back in the days, the field is limited to its employment on a circuit and other electronic equipment; now, in the modern world, the application of a "reverse" methodology includes almost anything – from children's toys and household appliances to neuroscience, computer programming, and DNA.

XIV.B. - Reasons for Reversing

One of the privileges that reverse engineering can grant to a circuit creator is the guarantee that a device is made accordingly. In the event that he chooses to base his circuit project on another circuit that was created with *questionable privacy*, he can determine any unethical practices. If he takes apart all of its components, he has the chance to have an insider look; by then, he can confirm whether unregulated modifications are in place.

Why use reverse engineering techniques for circuit-creation:

- Documentation purposes – especially in the case of shortcomings and low-quality circuit documentation, the diagnosis of a circuit is necessary to present new information

- Interfacing – with reverse engineering techniques can be subjected to interfacing; it can be evaluated accordingly, regarding its compatibility with another circuit

- Bug fixing – if there are critical faults in a circuit's design, it can be recognized better with a closer look at each of its components; instead of resorting to assumptions, a circuit creator can identify which part of his project needs modification

- Advanced technical information – advanced technical information is rewarded when opening up a circuit; especially for beginners, reverse engineering is a practical way of learning about the straightforward details within the system

- Incorporation of a new functionality – reverse engineering can allow the incorporation of a feature in a circuit; rather than design another circuit, a circuit creator can simply make modifications on his current project

- Modernization – reversing is beneficial in circuitry since it can be used to modernize a project; for instance, if most modern devices are popular in the market due to an innovative feature, a circuit creator can employ reverse engineering to add the same feature to his circuit

- Guarantee product security – if a circuit creator is unsure of the security of his project, reverse engineering is a way for him to determine certain concerns; he can check the specifications of each component and guarantee that none poses safety risks when put to use

XIV.C. – Is Reverse Engineering Similar to Hacking?

Since it is the method for the extraction of information on a circuit that can't be retrieved ordinarily, reverse engineering is argued to be a form of *corrupt hacking*; it is, therefore, a field that a few others in the electronics industry attempt to avoid. However, for many number of circuit engineers (as well as other engineers), there is brilliance in the entire concept of reverse engineering.

According to those who are not against the field, reverse engineering is a way of outsmarting an already finished product; additionally, as they would insist, isn't the point of engineering exactly that – to build and re-build until satisfying outcome is achieved? It may be considered as a form of hacking, but many contest to the idea that it is behind corrupt objectives.

XIV.D. – The Construction of Reverse Engineered Projects

Inarguably, reverse engineering is rather *destructive* and *invasive*. Some are not in favor of it since they do not welcome the idea of tearing their works apart. For others, however, it is a creative way of improving an already completed project; especially if the particular project is outstanding, they are granted the chance to make it even more outstanding.

Among the common projects that can be modified with the use of reverse engineering are *alarm clock radios, coffee machines,* and *colored lamps.* Alongside, the knowledge of internal systems, they can add a unique functionality that is not included during commercial distribution. For instance, you can add a new beeping sound to an alarm clock radio.

For the construction of various reverse engineering projects, it's advised to have a set of tools handy. Prepare a set of *screwdrivers, magnifiers,* and cutting equipment. Additionally, when the disassembly is completed, have a pack of *electrical tape* nearby.

Reverse engineering project tips for beginners:

- Take pictures of a circuit's front and back system prior to disassembly; you can use it as reference

- List down the set of procedures you plan on following; make sure you adhere to them

XIV.E. - Reverse Engineering & CAD

Reverse engineering rode along with the popularity of *CAD or Computer-Aided Design.* Through the years, the field that used to be limited to the basic improvement of a circuit's system began incorporating complex features. It provides a circuit creator the chance to analyze the internal portion of a device.

Moreover, instead of settling on getting a fundamental view of a circuit project that requires reverse engineering, a circuit creator can meticulously analyze a circuit; he can inspect each component thoroughly and come up at the most practical solution. For its development, circuit engineers, circuit designers, and other professionals on electronics started collaborative works with *architects* and those who are skilled in CAD.

Advantages of using CAD technology for a circuit project:

- To improve the alignment of each circuit component

- To enhance the designation of spaces within a circuit's system

- To modify geometric subjects for boosted performance

- To zoom in (and look closely) on each circuit component

XIV.F. - The Legality of the Industry

In light to the different discussions regarding its similarity to *corrupt hacking*, the reverse engineering industry is subjected to various legal complaints. There are even laws (that usually fall under contract laws and fraudulent manufacturing laws) meant for the protection of all sectors that employ *reversed* circuits or electronic devices.

The term *interoperability* is introduced in relation to a variety of legality concerns. With the emergence of cases that revolve around the disassembly of circuit's parts to compromise the quality of a circuit, some who tackle reverse engineered project are not received well.

Reverse engineering is, therefore, only considered illegal if the primary goal is to achieve interoperability. If the goal is for the improvement of a circuit's overall performance, it is encouraged; along with almost every other means of repairing a system, it is even recommended to arrive at a desired purpose.

Chapter XV – Hacking the System

Different communities of hackers host events that give light to those who are passionate in circuitry.

One community, *Artisan Asylum,* hosts a circuit hacking night once a week. In the gathering, circuit engineering fellows – from beginners to professionals, come together to discuss various concepts in circuitry and electronics. There, like-minded individuals share their love for circuitry and talk about their favorite projects, and basically, anything in the world of circuitry.

Moreover, Artisan Asylum's circuit hacking night provides great learning opportunities for circuit hacking enthusiasts. It presents lessons on how to solder, how to use particular computer programs, and how to modify a circuit to function as desired. Apart from teaching individuals the basics and advanced techniques on how to hack a circuit, and have it work as desired, the community encourages the attendees to think outside of the box and come up with brilliant and innovative ideas.

XV.A. – About Circuit Hacking

Circuit hacking, since it is linked with the word *hacking,* can sometimes be perceived as fraudulent. However, there is nothing fraudulent with it since the main reason why there are circuit hackers is for the improvement or the revision of a project; hacking, in this essence, is defined as the modification of an existing circuit to use it for a different purpose. And, in most cases, a circuit hacker is an individual who exhibits cleverness, open-mindedness, and technical aptness.

Due to a few similar concepts, circuit hacking and reverse engineering are said to be one and the same; they are not. While both may include certain techniques that are intended for the improvement of a circuit's operations, the former is merely focused on developing an existing circuit; it may be invasive, too, but it doesn't involve the *deconstruction of an entire circuit.* Especially if it was determined that the installment of a particular component can achieve a desired functionality, having to tear apart the other sections of a circuit is deemed unnecessary.

Common circuit hacking methods:

- Patching – a simple circuit hacking method that describes identifying a circuit's control mechanism or the most integral part of a circuit. Once the main component is identified, you can install a new and better component

- Component replacement – it is defined as replacing at least one component of a circuit with another component that comes with better quality

XV.B. – A Hacker's Main Tool: FIB Technology

FIB or *Focused Ion Beam* Technology is considered as one of a hacker's main tool since it grants him the chance to hack almost any circuit. Ever since the initial introduction of the applications in the 1990s, their usefulness hadn't come unappreciated. The early versions were not only quite expensive, but also, clearly, in need of improvement; later, the tools underwent continuous modifications from many electronics enthusiasts.

According to a study that was led by the engineers at Berlin Technical University, a person skilled in circuitry can install FIB Technology-based applications to hack into a system's security. For the particular research, an IC with low-level security was the focus; the objective was to work around its level of security with the goal of deliberately eliminating its defensive mechanism. The study was, of course, successful and eventually, it was proven that even high-level tools can be hacked with the same practice. And, as it follows, it sheds light on the concept that *there is no such thing as a tamper-proof circuit.*

Moreover, FIB Technology, as a clever technique of manufacturing, developing, and re-wiring a circuit, has earned the approval of different communities of hackers and circuit engineers. Alongside its advantage of boosting a system's performance, it reduces regular operation time. Due to its ingenious way of allowing an individual who's working on an electronic device to design (and even re-design repeatedly) his project, it was subjected to further developments.

Important parts of applications that incorporate FIB Technology (as shown in the layout):

- Aperture – it is in charge of gathering visual aids, then, modifying these tools for a clear display of retrievable information from a particular electronic device

- Deflector plates – it accepts, interprets, then, measures receivable data; initially, it acknowledges all information prior to the screening of the unnecessary ones

- Extractor – it is in charge of drawing out information from an electronic device, then, transferring them to the hacking mechanism

- Lens – it is in charge of making adjustments to assist when processing information

- Octupoles – it is also known as double quadrupoles or octopoles, which means something that has eight poles; it controls beams of ions

- Suppressor – it is designed to prevent power overload due to voltage spikes; it works by regulating the amount of electric current within a system so a device can remain functional

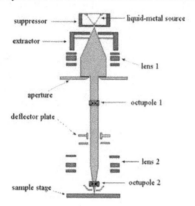

The installment of FIB Technology can be very promising to a hacker

Functions of applications that incorporate FIB Technology:

- Enable and/or disable intruder detection

- Evaluate a circuit's behavior

- Evaluate a circuit's defects

- Gather secret codes and security keys

- Obtain personal details, sensitive data, and proprietary information

- Remove protection systems (e.g. tamper networks, trace meshes, optical sensors, etc.)

- Route incoming data to be received by another network

- Trace and re-trace changes

XV.C. – Circuit Hacking Project

A plus side to the knowledge of how a circuit operates is that you can choose any from your pack of electronic devices and have it upgraded according to preference; the possibilities of its new functions are endless. You won't even have to spend a grand amount, so long as you're familiar with the functions of particular installments. The result of hacking the original system may be rather bizarre, since the product is no longer the same, but nonetheless, the result is likely the way you desired.

In the sample project below, the goal is hack a charger; particularly, modify an existing charger and have it operate with a battery. It can be connected to any electronic device with a USB port. This is useful during emergencies when an electric outlet is nowhere to be found.

Project example (derived from http://www.maximumpc.com): USB Charger with Battery

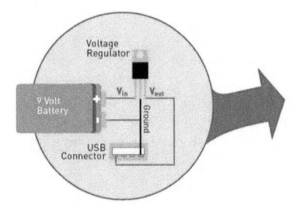

A USB charger with battery can be used for hours (depending on your voltage source)

Materials:

- Charger
- 5-volt voltage regulator
- 9-volt battery
- 9-volt battery clip
- Electrical tape

- USB connector

- Copper wire

Procedures (as shown in the layout above):

1. On a side of the charger, drill a hole for the placement of the USB connector.

2. On the other side of the charger, drill a hole for the placement of the 5-volt voltage regulator.

3. At the bottom center (between the 2 holes), place the 9-volt battery.

4. Above it, establish a ground using the copper wire and 9-volt battery clip.

5. Solder the components together.

6. Wrap the product with electrical tape.

Chapter XVI – Advanced Circuit Engineering: Microcontrollers & Robots

Among the plethora of prospects for a circuit engineer is the opportunity to engage in *circuit-bending* or the art (and science) of modifying existing circuits of electronic devices, and turning them into new musical instruments. In many cases, he isn't required to follow a set of rules for *tweaking* a circuit to incorporate a particular sound; in fact, he can re-design an electronic device as desired.

Alongside, an advantage of circuit-bending is its reward of reducing necessary expenses. In the event that he is very resourceful, the circuit creator can maximize the advantage even more; he can install used (but in working condition) components or less costly parts.

Circuit-bending is merely one of the exciting possibilities for a fellow in circuitry. The options are rather limitless, especially if you let your creativity run loose. So long as you are certain that a circuit will work given a particular arrangement, you shouldn't hold back in taking your beginner's knowledge of circuits to an advanced level.

XVI.A. – A Circuit Engineer's Future in Robotics & Computer Engineering

A reward of being skilled in circuitry is the opportunity to venture into other engineering fields such as *robotics engineering* and *computer engineering*. Your knowledge of how a circuit operates? You can look at it from a brand new perspective; you don't have to be simply in the industry of circuit engineering or electronics engineering. Apart from its offer of a more bountiful career; you can employ it to create a project (or a batch of projects) that you can be proud of. With the mastery of the basic circuitry lessons, delving into related fields becomes easier and more exciting.

With your interest in circuitry, you may seek for other career positions; usually, the employers of robotics engineers and computer engineers welcome circuit engineers into their workforce due to *trainability, familiarity with circuits,* and *good background in electronics.* It may take another set of years of studying, along with new skills to learn, but you can definitely go higher; it takes commitment from your end, too.

Advanced lessons that will be useful for a circuit engineer:

- Integral connections for hardware components

- Software and hardware essentials

- Robotic essentials

- Computer operations

- Computer architecture

- Computer programming (recommended programming languages are C and C++)

XVI.B. – Microcontroller + Microcontroller Programming

A *microcontroller* is a small device that serves as the computer in a circuit; it is a common tool that can be found in *remote controls, smart medical assistance equipment, office machines, state-of-the-art appliances,* and *engine control systems.* With the rapid pace of various information-retrieval operations, its function of addressing *size, cost, time,* and *performance* concerns offers privileges a user with improved overall performance. It is usually implanted on a separate electronic device before or after that device is finished. In certain cases, it uses 4-bit words and low frequency clock-rate operations.

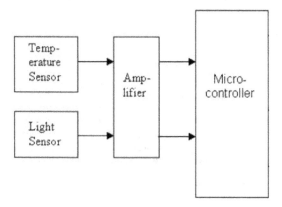

A microcontroller is dependent on a programmer's instructions

Moreover, while a microcontroller is a very useful device, it is only as good as the program that was written for it; this is where the importance of *microcontroller programming* enters the picture. It is a tool that merely executes certain instructions; in the absence of specific commands, it won't function. However, if you design it with even a hundred task capabilities, it can perform each one without fault; granted it was programmed well, it can power a device as desired.

What a microcontroller can do:

- Enable and/or disable clock feature
- Enable and/or disable light capabilities
- Configure audio and video settings
- Add an external monitor
- Automatically detect and/or repair errors
- Automatically update old components
- Magnify an electronic device's performance
- Eliminate unwanted features
- Tighten security features

Example of microcontroller programming:

Result	Microcontroller Programming (in C language)

By tweaking its USB components, a microcontroller's clock setting can be formatted. It is also programmed to activate BL or backlight with a trigger.	for (;;) [
	
	handleserial ();
	
	CDC_USBdevice (&interface)
	
	CDC_USBdevice (&digitalizer)
	
	handleserial ();
	
	]
	
	]
	
	/Setup/ [
	
	int ret
	
	USB_initialize
	
	clock_setup (div1);
	
	BL_off (1), BL_on (0);
	
	ret = digitizer_USB_initialize ();

	if (ret)

XVI.C. – Robots + Robotics

Another way that you can take your knowledge in circuitry up a notch is to consider a career in *robotics engineering*. Due to your familiarity with a circuit, you can begin honing your skills in creating coherent circuits; you can construct a series that is dependent on the individual circuits to deliver its primary function.

As you commit to robotics, like in programming, a lineup of new skills (e.g. artificial intelligence developments, dynamics, motion planning techniques, mapping tactics, etc.) must be acquired, too. This time, other than your hand in circuits and other electronic components, you have to visit aspects in the *mechanical* fields. However, given your exposure to similar concepts in circuitry, learning in the field may not be a challenge.

With your expertise in circuits, you can be behind innovative and extraordinary robotics projects that can be advantageous for both commercial and personal use. It just takes a matter of determination to move forward, and the fact remains that a course in circuit engineering can present you with a satisfying place in robotics, as well as other promising opportunities.

Conclusion

Thank you again for purchasing this book!

I hope this book was able to help you understand the fundamentals in circuit engineering. The lessons shared to you here are meant for a beginner in the subject; the different discussions are written simply. And, so far, it may have dawned on you that there's still more to discover about circuits.

The next step is to learn even more about circuitry and circuit engineering. Especially if you're considering a career in the field, advanced lessons would be good. Since this book has introduced you to the subject, and maybe inspired you to see the fun side in circuits, as well as electronics and electrical engineering, you may want to take the beginner's perspective to a whole other level.

Finally, if you enjoyed this book, please take the time to share your thoughts and post a review on Amazon. It'd be greatly appreciated!

Thank you and good luck!

Book 2

Human-Computer Interaction

By Solis Tech

The Fundamentals Made Easy!

Human-Computer Interaction: The Fundamentals Made Easy!

Table of Contents

Introduction

I want to thank you and congratulate you for purchasing the book, "Human-Computer Interaction: The Fundamentals Made Easy!"

This book contains proven steps and strategies on how to conceptualize and design a computer system that incorporate principles on effective interaction between the user and the device.

Human-computer interaction (HCI) is the study of the interaction between people and computers and the degree at which computers are developed enough to successfully interact with humans. So many institutions particularly academic and corporations now study HCI. Unfortunately, ease-of-use has not been a priority to most computer systems developer. The issue continues to bedevil the HCI community as accusations still abound that computer makers are still indifferent and are not making enough effort to make truly user-friendly products.

On the other hand, the designing task of computer system developers is not simple either as computers are very complex products. It is also true that the demand for use of computers have grown by leaps and bounds outstripping the need for ease-of-use by a significant margin. If you are a computer designer or simply have basic interest in making devices more effective for users, this book will help you a lot.

Thanks again for purchasing this book, I hope you enjoy it!

Chapter 1: Aspects of HCI

Main aspects of HCI

HCI is composed of three main features, namely: the user, the computer, and their interaction or how they work together.

"User" refers to either the individual or the group of users doing things together. An understanding of how the people's sense of sight, hearing, and touch send information is very important. Also, the type of mental models of interactions differs according to the personality of the user. And finally, interactions are also influenced by cultural and national differences.

"Computer," on the other hand, pertains to all technology from desktop to huge computer systems. As an example, if the topic is website design, the computer would then be the website. "Computers" would also include gadgets like mobile phones or even VCRs.

Finally, the "Interaction" is what happens as "User" uses the "Computer" to achieve a certain objective. Humans, of course, are totally different from machines. So the HCI's main intent is to ensure a successful interaction between the two.

In this aspect, adequate knowledge about humans and computers are critical to realize a functioning system. You need to seek inputs from users. Such knowledge would provide much needed information in determining schedule and budget that are crucial to the systems. In effect there are ideal situations and perfect systems. But the key is finding the balance between what is ideal and what is really feasible given the existing situation.

Objectives of HCI

HCI aims to come up with systems that are functional, usable, and safe. Developing computer systems with excellent usability depends on:

- having enough understanding of the aspects that lead people to use technology in certain ways
- being able to devise tools and ways for creating suitable systems
- the development of safe, effective, and efficient interaction

- making people the priority

The main philosophy underneath HCI is that the users or the people using the computers always come first. Developers must always be guided by the users' needs and preferences in designing systems. It is the system that should match the requirements of human users and not people changing to suit the nature of the machines.

The primacy of usability

Usability is one of the principal considerations in HCI. It is simply about ensuring that a system can be easily learned and used or be what is called user-friendly. A system is considered usable if it:

- can be learned easily
- can be remembered easily in terms of use
- is effective
- is efficient
- is safe
- is enjoyable

Lack of usability means wasted time, mistakes, and disappointments. Unfortunately, a lot of existing systems and devices have been designed without sufficient attention to usability. These include ATM, the Web, computer, printer, mobile phone, personal organizer, coffee machine, remote control, soft drink machine, ticket machine, photocopier, stereo, watch, video game, library information systems, and calculator.

A good example is the photocopier. If you are not familiar with the symbols on the buttons you will be greatly confused. For instance, the big button with the C on it actually refers to Clear, not Copy. The button used to produce copies is actually on the left side with an unrelated symbol. Devices and gadgets should be easy, effortless, and enjoyable to use.

Analyzing and designing a system based on HCI principles involve a lot of factors that produce really complex analysis because of interactions among many of them. The major factors are:

- The User – motivation, satisfaction, experience, enjoyment, personality. Also cognitive processes and capabilities

- User Interface – navigation, output devices, icons, commands, input devices, graphics, dialogue structures, user support, use of color, multimedia, natural language
- Environmental Factors – health and safety, noise, heating, lighting, ventilation
- Organization Factors – job design, work organization, training, roles, politics
- Task Factors – task allocation, skills, easy, novel, complex, monitoring
- Comfort Factors – seating, layout, equipment
- Constraints – budgets, buildings, cost, equipment, timescales, staff
- Productivity Factors – decrease costs, increase quality, increase innovation, increase output, decrease errors
- System Functionality – software, hardware, application

There are different disciplines representing a wide array of subjects that are covered in HCI. The manifold inputs from these fields have continued to enrich HCI. The disciplines include:

- Cognitive Psychology – limitations, performance predictions, information processing, cooperative working, capabilities
- Ergonomics – display readability, hardware design
- Computer Science – graphics, software design, prototyping tools, technology, User Interface Management Systems (UIMS) and User Interface Development Environments (UIDE)
- Social Psychology – social and organizational structures
- Engineering and Design – engineering principles, graphic designs
- Linguistics – natural language interfaces
- Philosophy, Sociology, and Anthropology – computer supported cooperative work (CSCW)
- Artificial Intelligence – intelligent software

Chapter 2: The Human Side in the HCI

Some of the key aspects that shed light on the human side of HCI are:

1. Perceptual-Motor Interaction. Effective human-computer interface design requires an appreciation of the whole human perceptual-motor system. The information-processing approach is central to the perceptual-motor behavior study and for considering the human factors in HCI. An effective interface design reflects the designer's knowledge of the perceptual such as visual displays, use of sound, and graphics. Also the cognitive exemplified by conceptual models and desktop metaphors as well as motoric constraints like ergonomic keyboards of the human perpetual-motor system.

   Man has gone beyond the use of computer punch cards and command-line interfaces. We now use speech recognition, eye-gaze control, and graphical user interfaces. The importance of various perceptual, cognitive, and motor constraints of the human system is now better recognized in HCI. An effective interface must take into account the perceptual and action expectations of users, the action that is seen with a response location, and the mapping of the perceptual-motor workspaces.

2. Human Information Processing. Aspects of human information processing such as models, theories, and methods are currently well developed. The available knowhow in this field is broadly useful to HCI in general such as in the representation and communication of knowledge and visual display design. An effective HCI requires making the interaction compatible with the human information-processing capabilities. Many things about human information processing have been integrated into cognitive architectures that are now applicable to HCI. These applications include the Model Human Processor, the Act model, the SOAR model, and the Epic model.

3. Mental Models in Human–Computer Interaction. Studying mental models can help understand HCI by inspecting the processes by which such models impact behavior. For example, mental models of machines can enable both novice and seasoned problem solvers to find new methods for fulfilling a task through more elaborate encoding of remembered methods.

   The Reverse Polish Notation is a great example of this. There is also a general theory that says readers develop a representation in their mind at several levels of what they read. First is the encoding of text, followed by the representation of propositional content of text. Finally, to this text, they integrate world knowledge to form a mental model of the situation described.

Readers also have the ability to look for ideas in multiple texts. They construct a kind of structured mental maps that show which documents contained which ideas even when they did not expect to need it while reading. Mental models are generally considered as semantic knowledge. Focusing on the degree of commonality among team members, for instance, when it comes to knowledge and beliefs, allows quantitative measures of similarity and differences which is the language of computers.

4. Emotion in Human–Computer Interaction. Emotion used to be persona non grata in the field of computer design. It had no place in the efficiency and rationality of computers which were the personification of zero emotion. Recent study findings in the field of psychology and technology show in a totally different light the relationship between humans, computers, and emotions.

Emotion has ceased to be considered only in light of anger generated by inexplicable computer crashes or hyper excitement caused by video games. Nowadays, it is widely accepted that a host of emotions are important part of computer-related activities such as Web search, sending an email, online shopping, and playing computer games. In almost everything now, the emotional systems get engaged according to psychologists.

Studies and discussions on emotion and computers have grown a lot because of dramatic advances in technology. Computers have actually been used to evaluate the relationship between emotion and its correlates. In the same vein, the astounding improvements in quality and speed of signal processing now enable computers to form conclusion on a user's emotional condition. Compared to purely textual interfaces that have very limited range, the multimodal interfaces that can use voices, faces, and bodies are now more capable to a broader range of emotions.

Nowadays, the performance of an interface will be seriously impeded without considering the user's emotional state. Surprisingly, it can earn even descriptions like socially inept, incompetent, and cold. Much remains to be done to successfully incorporate emotion recognition into interfaces. Still, more studies about the interaction between design and testing can help create interfaces that are efficient and effective while providing satisfaction and enjoyment.

5. Cognitive Architecture. A cognitive architecture is a computer simulation program that makes use of human cognition principle based on human experimental data. It also refers to software artifacts developed by computer programmers. Likewise, the term also includes large software systems which are considered hard to develop and maintain.

Right now, cognitive architectures are not widely utilized by HCI practitioners. Nevertheless, it is quite relevant as an engineering field to usability and has important applications in computing systems especially in HCI. It also serves as theoretical science in human computer interaction studies. Finally, cognitive architectures combine artificial intelligence methods and knowledge with data and principles from cognitive psychology.

Presently-known cognitive architectures are undergoing improvements and are being utilized in HCI-related tasks. Two of the most well-known systems, EPIC and ACT, are production systems or built around one. All systems have production rules which differ from architecture to architecture. The difference lies on focus and history although there's a certain similarity in intellectual history. They may have more congruence than differences at some levels either because of mutual borrowings or due to the convergence of the science. The third system, Soar, is a bit different than the first two production system models.

The three production systems, Soar, Epic, and ACT-R were developed to present different types of human cognition but showed more similarities than divergence as they developed. It is not easy to describe a value possessed by architecture as advantage because to others it constitutes a disadvantage. For instance, Soar's learning mechanism is very important for modeling the improvement of users for a period of time. But there are many applications also where Soar's features result to harmful side effects that can cause more difficulty in model construction.

6. Task Loading and Stress in HCI. Stress in the form of task loading is central to HCI. The traditional perspective on stress sees it in light of exposure to some adverse environmental situations such as noise and the focus of attention centers on most affected physiological system. A new way of looking at it, however, stems from the findings that all stress effects are mediated through the brain.

And since the brain is mainly focused on ongoing behavior or current task, stress ceases to be a peripheral issue but that the ongoing task becomes the primary source of stress. And this renders stress concerns that are central to all HCI issues. This means computer-based systems which aim at helping people lessen cognitive workload and task complexity actually impose more burdens and stress on them.

The person's coping mechanism for such stress affects their work performance and personal wellbeing. The environment may vary but some mechanisms for appraising stress in all task demands are the same. So for HCI, certain principles and designs for stress are applicable across multiple domains.

There are several theories of stress and performance and their connection to human-computer interaction. Workload and stress are at times considered as varying perspectives on the same problem. There are some general practices for stress mitigation. But quite important for this topic is setting up effective measures of information processing and mental resources. It also includes expounding on task dimensions that are relevant and their relationship to self-regulatory mechanisms.

It is critical to establish how an individual's appraisal of his/her environment can be influenced by personal traits and states. This is because stress can only be understood vis-a-vis interaction between a person and the environment. Lastly, it is better to treat stress at multiple levels whether physiological or organizational when making practical application. Instead of one-dimensional which is bound to fail, multidimensional is better as it considers the person, task, and the physical, social and organizational environments.

The implication is that HCI researchers and practitioners should go beyond the design of interface displays and controls and focus also on the person aspects. What are the things in the individual that affect performance and the physical-social environment where the human-technology interaction happens? It means that the technical principles at work in that situation are not adequate. They cannot develop a complete description of the relationship between resources and cognitive activities.

7. Motivating, Influencing, and Persuading Users. From its former role as tool for scientists, the spread of computer use to all sectors of society has brought new uses for computers. Among those uses are persuading people to change their attitudes and behavior. Nowadays, it is widely accepted that skills in motivating and persuading people are necessary for developing a successful HCI.

Interaction designers are actually agents of influence which unfortunately they have not yet understood and applied. Yet their works often involve creating something that tries to change people though they may not be conscious of it. Among these works are motivating people to register the software, learn an online application, or have product loyalty. Changing people's attitudes is now a common feature in the success of interactive products.

Depending on the types of product, the persuasion factor can either be small or large. At any rate, anything that needs to be marketed needs to be persuasive. The growing use of computing products and the limitless scalability of software makes interaction designers one of the best potential change agents in the future.

Take for example the Web-interaction designers who increasingly are facing more challenge in designing something that will hold the attention and motivation of information seekers. After that, they need to persuade web users to adopt certain behaviors like:

- using a software
- joining a survey
- clicking on the ads
- returning often after bookmarking a site
- buying things online
- releasing personal information
- forming an online community

Being able to persuade people is a measure of success here. But with success comes responsibility. The Web designer needs to make the website credible. The following are some broad guidelines to ensure credibility:

1. Design websites to present the real and practical aspects of the organization.
2. Invest sufficiently in visual design
3. Make websites that people can easily use.
4. Include markers of good quality
5. Use markers of reliability.
6. Avoid too much commercialism on a website
7. Adopt and adjust to the user experience
8. Avoid being amateurish

To sum it all, computer systems have become an inescapable part of everyday life. The interactive experience involving all systems be it mobile phone or desktop can be designed in such a way as to influence the way we think and act. By combining the computing capability with persuasion psychology, computer systems can motivate and persuade. Humans are undoubtedly still superior when it comes to influencing people. But in many areas of endeavor, computer can do what humans cannot even imagine being capable of.

Computers don't sleep and can be designed to keep trying on and on. At the very least, computers provide a new way for modifying how people act and think. Like it or not, the community of HCI professionals is at the forefront of the campaign to make more sensitive and responsive tech products. It can rise to the challenge of helping churn out products that enhance the people's over-all quality of life. Or it can continue being a tool to produce mindless products whose main reason for being into is to make profit for the owners.

8. Human-Error Identification in Human–Computer Interaction. The leap from focusing on human error in technological problems to a less obvious culprit started in the 1940's. It was established during that year that plane pilot error was often designer error. It began to show that design is the key to

substantially reduce human error and this paradigm continued to gather steam particularly in HCI.

It is now common wisdom that human error can be as often as the product of a defective design or as a person making a mistake. The inadequate design fosters activities that lead to errors. A groundbreaking outcome of this new philosophy is that errors are now viewed as totally predictable events instead of seeing it as unpredictable occurrences. This makes errors avoidable.

So errors became instances where planned series of steps and activities fail to realize intended results independent of any outside change agencies. If errors are no longer random, then it can be identified and predicted ahead of time. What partially drove this line of thinking are the accidents that happened in the nuclear industry that is hungry for preemptive solutions. This has led to the formulation of several human-error identification (HEI) techniques.

Although evaluative and summative in nature, these HEI techniques that employ ergonomics methods can now be used in formative design stages especially in analytic prototyping. For instance, the entry of computer-aided design such as in architecture has profound impacts on prototyping. It made possible what was considered as impossible or too prohibitively costly design alteration at the structural prototyping stage.

The three main forms of prototyping human interfaces have been identified namely: functional analysis, scenario analysis, and structural analysis.

Functional analysis includes consideration of the functional range supported by the device. In comparison, scenario analysis is exemplified by consideration of the device in relation to events sequence. An example of the structural analysis, on the other hand, is the use of user-centered viewpoint in a non-destructive testing of the interface.

One compelling example of the crucial role of design in predicting and minimizing errors concern human error identification (HEI) tools like the TAFEI or Task Analysis for Error Identification. The results of the application of TAFEI on interface project designs show how it can improve systems and its relevance to other ergonomic methods. It served to validate what has been long suspected when it comes to error-design relationship as follow:

- Structured systems like TAFEI results to reliable and trustworthy error data;

- Most errors resulting from technology are totally predictable;

- To improve design and reduce errors, ergonomics methods should be employed in formative design process.

Exploring design weaknesses through tools like TAFEI will go a long way in developing and producing devices and gadgets that are tolerant to error.

Chapter 3: The Computer Side in the HCI

The salient points when it comes to the computer side in HCI include:

1. <u>Input Technologies and Techniques</u>. Input devices which are also a classification of computer can detect physical aspects of places, things, and, of course, people. However, its function is never complete without considering the visual feedback corresponding to the input. It is like using a writing instrument without something to write on. Input and output should always go together.

   And in devices with small screens, this is only possible with the help of integrated sensors. If the user or human characteristics are important in a maximized HCI environment, so are input technologies with enough sophistication to meet user-machine interaction requirements. Users can only achieve the task objectives by combining the right feedback with inputs. In this regard, the HCI designer should take into account the following:

a. the industrial and ergonomic design of the gadget

b. the physical censor

c. the relationship among all interaction techniques

Input gadgets have many properties that apply to the usual pointing devices or mobile items with touch input. These pointing devices include the: mice, trackballs, isometric joysticks, isotonic joysticks, indirect tablets, touchpads, touchscreens, and pen-operated devices. The mice or mouse, of course, is one of the most popular as anyone who has ever used a computer knows. Because of its inherent advantages for individual users where it can easily be used by most people, it is one of the most preferred pointing devices.

Touchpads are most well-known to laptop users. These are small tablets that are sensitive to touch and which are usually featured on laptop units. Touchscreens on the other hand are tablets that are sensitive to touch which are placed on a display. It is increasingly becoming the tool to beat because of the proliferation of smart phones and other hand-held devices.

There are input models and theories that are quite helpful in evaluating the efficacy of interaction strategies. But it would be most beneficial to readers here to focus on current and future trends for this feature. Interactive system designers should go beyond the usual things like graphical user interface and pointing ideas when it comes to inputs.

They must delve deeper into more effective search strategies, sensor inputs for new data types, and techniques of synthesis to make much better sense of data. Better search tools will enhance navigation and manual search regarding file systems. One outstanding development is the breakthrough in the development of more advanced sensor inputs such as technologies for tagging and location.

It allows computers to identify physical objects and locations that have been tagged, and to detect their location and distance to other devices through signal strength analysis. These sensors are making interface personalization much easier. This development in interaction also has great implications for data mining and techniques for machine learning. Continuous improvement in structure synthesis and extraction techniques is invaluable in this data-rich era.

An overriding aim in HCI is to achieve dramatic advancement in humanity's interaction with technology. The computer side of this presents limitless possibilities but the cognitive skills and senses of man will be relatively stagnant. Our holding, touching, and object-movement are not the result of technology-like progress but a product of our human limitations.

2. Recognition- and Sensor-Based Input for Interaction. Computers are able to manipulate physical signals that have been transformed by sensors into electrical signals. Sensors have found their way into various fields of industry such as robotics, automotive, and aerospace. It has also found vast applications in consumer products.

The computer mouse is a very good example. Imagine that simple-looking device equipped with algorithms that process images and specialized camera that enables it to be unbelievably sensitive to motions. It detects movement at the rate of a thousand of an inch several thousand times per second. Another interesting device is the accelerometer that detects acceleration due to movement and continuous acceleration because of gravity.

Digital cameras now make use of accelerometers to save a photo. Laptops also are equipped with accelerometers for self-protection. When the laptop is accidentally dropped the accelerometer enables the hard disk to secure the hard drive prior to impact. With smartphones, the goal is for motion sensing for the purpose of interaction such as determining the walking pattern of users. Generally, HCI research on sensors dwells on its usage to improve interaction.

Sensor studies are either to broaden input options or build new computing forms. The new forms include mobile devices that recognize locations and places that are sensitive to the presence and needs of its inhabitants. Still there are far more advanced goals and applications like in robotics.

There is a race to develop machines that will behave and think like humans or at least complement their capabilities. It has many critical applications such as in nuclear power accident mitigation. One worry, of course, is that it will end up in the military. But in safety, mobile computing, entertainment, productivity, affective computing, and surveillance, sensors are finding widespread application.

An intriguing side note here is the idea of developing a sensor to enable computers to detect and accordingly react to the frustration of its user. The computer's response could be something like playing relaxing music. Sensing could be in the form of the user banging on the keyboard in frustration. A microphone could react to the yelling of the speaker or the webcam could sense scowling.

In general, the potential of interactive sensing is quite good. The degree of progress across the whole computing spectrum actually gives the impression that sky is the limit. Advances in nanotechnology, CPU power, and storage capacities will continue to produce more outstanding innovations in the computer side of HCI.

But what is driving the unprecedented growth of the sensor-based interactive systems is the dizzying expansion in devices outside the old desktop computer. It is hard to keep track of the explosive proliferation of smart phones, tablet PCs, portable gaming devices, music and movie players, living room-centric computers, and personal digital assistants. Computing is becoming part and parcel of our daily life and our environment.

Through recognition techniques and sensing systems, task-specific computing devices will be developed instead of general functions. It will also pave the way for different types of interaction style in HCI. This activity-specific interactive systems development will further hasten innovations on a much broader array of practical applications.

3. Visual Displays. Timekeeping has always been one function that man has strived for a good visual display. Today's smartwatches which are actually wrist computers sport stunning visual displays. It is no longer limited to displaying time but is multifunctional. Some brands can pinpoint exact location in the planet through a global positioning system. Others can show heart rate while a number can be personal digital assistants.

The main idea behind wearable computing is that the human body is wearing the visual displays. One major way people use wearables is to put the display on one's head making user's hands free to work. It is called headmounted displays or HMDs. The screen-based is one category of HMDs. It makes use of the retinal-projection method which projects images on the retina of the eye.

An alternative method is the scanning displays which scan images onto the retina pixel by pixel. A second type of display which is actually much bigger in scope and the most widespread is the hand-held and wrist-worn displays. They are in mobile phones, media players, wristwatches, and other portable gadgets. Apple is one of the global leaders in this field and the most well-known. Even textiles for clothing are now being used for such technology in what is now known as photonic textiles-fabric.

Multicolored lighting systems were merged with the fabrics for its electronic information function without affecting the cloth's softness. It has sensors, GSM, and Bluetooth! Photonic fabrics have great promising applications in the areas of personal health care and communication.

4. Haptic Interfaces. Haptic interface refers to a device for sending feedback that produces sensation of weight, touch, rigidity, and other aspects through the skin and muscle. This force feedback mechanism is designed to enhance computer-human interaction. Because haptics are done through actual physical contact, they are not easy to synthesize unlike the sense of sight and sound that are gathered through the eyes and ears.

The genius in the haptic interface is that it simply makes use of the body's own highly sophisticated receptor system. The haptic feedback is made possible through synthetic stimulation in the skin and proprioception.

Proprioception involves something deeper than the skin – the muscle and skeleton. The mechanoreceptors in the body enable its detection of contact forces received from the environment. Body receptors sense velocity, skin stretching, vibration, and edges of objects. Haptic interfaces are more widely applied in the field of virtual reality than in information media and related devices are now available commercially.

Two of the most important research needs on haptic interfaces in the future concern the psychology in haptics and safety considerations. Safety is a crucial issue as insufficient actuator control can lead to injuries for users. Control problems may occur with the tool displays and exoskeleton. Unintended forces or vibration may pose danger to the user.

A locomotion interface that holds a user's body can cause serious physical damage if control is inadequate. It requires proven safety equipment that amply protects the walker and this should be a major objective of research. A much safer alternative is a system where the user does not wear any equipment during the interaction.

The psychology in haptics on the other hand requires more studies on muscle sensation as most existing findings are on skin sensation. Among the few promising findings relate to Laderman and Klatzky's work (1987) on force display and their recent study of forces distributed according to space. Their psychological findings have very promising applications in the development of haptic interface. A lot of obstacles need to be overcome before usage of haptic interface becomes widespread.

Though men cannot do without haptics in real life interaction, it is still of limited use in HCI. One can say haptic interface is still in infancy with its 10-year background. So eventually its time will come just like image displays (e.g. TV and movies) which started 100 years ago. For now, what are available are a few haptic interfaces with limited functionality and high cost. At the very least, haptic interface is a new very promising frontier in HCI with immense potential contribution to man's quality of life.

5. <u>Non-speech Auditory Output</u>. Sound is one of the key aspects that complete our interaction with our environment. But where speech is direct and necessitates focus and attention, non-speech sound is more diffused and provides a different class of information.

   Non-speech sounds include sounds from the environment, music, and sound effects. Nevertheless, speech and non-speech sounds complement each other just like text is complemented by visual symbols. Non-speech sounds can give information in a shorter period of time than speech.

   Right now, the non-speech field needs more research. The user interface is a much more effective tool for HCI when it employs a combined visual and sound feedback. This sound-visual combination has complementary function as well. Visual gives specific information about a small area reached by our eyes but sound or the auditory system provides more general information from beyond our focus.

   Our senses are the key to our effective interaction with the external world. These senses in turn bring more dimensions in information as they enhance one another. These principles are very useful in a multimodal HCI by adding non-speech sound output to the graphical displays. An example of this application is focusing our eyes on one task like editing a manuscript while monitoring other aspects in the machine through sound.

Reliance on visual sense which is more prevalent at present can be problematic. One problem is there could be visual overload which means the user could miss lots of information. Or simply that the viewer cannot look at everything at the same time at all times. Sound can help eliminate that situation by giving information to the user that the eyes could not see.

This interdependence between visual and audio could make information presentation far more efficient. Non-speech sound is mainly used in games' sound effects, music, and other multimedia usages. It is commonly employed in creating a certain mood for the item like in movies. In HCI, sound is used to provide information particularly those things that a user does not see or notice such as what is going on in their computer systems.

It is useful to use non-speech sound in HCI for many reasons. Seeing and hearing in the human body is first of all interdependent. The eyes can give information that is high-resolution only in a limited area of focus. But sounds can be received from all sides of the user: front, above, below, and behind. This not only provides direct information but also tells the eyes where to look to get more useful data. In fact, at times reaction to sound stimuli is faster than what is seen.

Non-speech sound can therefore help in reducing large display overload which can cause users to miss important data. This is especially true in large graphical interfaces that use multiple monitors. Using sound to present some information would reduce screen space. It would also lessen the volume of information that should be on the screen. This is most relevant to gadgets with small visual displays like smartphones and PDAs.

Non-speech sound would also decrease demands on our visual attention. For instance, a user who is walking would miss much information as he looks at his device's visual display because of competing attention from the traffic or uneven surface where he is walking. In fact, if the information is in sound, he does not have to look at his device at all.

Our sense of sound is also underutilized. Yet as exemplified by classical music, its intricate organization can make, say a symphony, a powerful tool for transmitting complex information. The beauty with sound is that it grabs attention. It is easy to avoid looking at something but hard to ignore sound which makes it very effective in sending important information. Likewise, certain things in the interface look more natural in sound than in sight.

Finally, non-speech sound will allow visually-impaired users to use computers. Newer graphical displays have, in particular, made it even harder for them to operate the device. Research has been extensive in the HCI application of non-speech sound in a wide range of topics.

There are two main areas of growth where the application of non-speech sound has the best potential. One is in the creation of multimodal displays that utilizes all available senses. This means integrating sound with other things like force-feedback and tactile apart from sight. The other area is in wearable and mobile computing gadgets that also use multimodal displays.

As mentioned, the screens of these devices are small and sound will reduce the need for screen space.

6. <u>Network-Based Interaction</u>. Networked interfaces have modified our perception of society and the world at large particularly with the Web and now mobile devices. There are several roles that networks play in HCI. The first is as an Enabler which refers to things that can be done only with network. The second is as Mediator which pertains to problems and issues caused by networks.

Third is as Subject which focuses on managing and understanding networks and fourth as Platform which dwells on interface architectures and algorithms. Network includes both the wire-based and the wireless world. Things are rapidly changing especially in the wireless networks. These changes can be classified in two dimensions, namely:

- **Global vs. Local** – refers to the distance by space between the connected points such as machines in the office to global networks like the Internet.

- **Fixed vs. Flexible** – pertains to the nature of the links between points such as fixed devices and gadget that configures itself. More changes are coming because of spreading wireless links. One example is being able to gain access to internet connections and printers of another office by simply plugging a portable device into the Ethernet.

Traditionally, LANs belong to local-fixed category while Internet is global-fixed. Hand-helds like cell phones are also categorized as global-fixed because phones are fixed and independent of location. The internet makes use of domain names which are fixed like URLs. Some phone technologies like GSM and GPRS are classified as global-fixed because it is possible to send content that is based on location. Also the enlarging data capability is enabling services to handle huge media content.

What set these technologies apart, however, are the connectivity model and the charging which are usually by data use or fixed charge. There are a number of current and new technologies from the local-flexible type. These include the Wi-Fi, infrared, Bluetooth, and ZigBee which permit flexible connections among personal gadgets. With them, a computer device can utilize a mobile-phone modem or a headset with Bluetooth can make connections with a phone, wireless. Unfortunately, these capabilities also enhance unsavory activities like illegal equipment accessing, hacking, and surveillance.

7. <u>Wearable Computers</u>. Computers have become like appendage to many office workers. But it is hard for those using mobile devices to get the information

they need. In a mobile situation, existing interfaces will hamper the user's main task. Users will be forced to prioritize the device instead of the environment. The need is for a wearables design that helps fulfill not obstruct the task.

A framework that can be very useful in creating good designs of computer interfaces which are wearable is CAMP. This framework addresses different factors that may impinge on the effectiveness of the design such as body closeness and how it is used. CAMP stands for:

- Corporal – which means absence of discomfort to users during physical interface with the wearable.
- Attention – interface design should allow user to focus both on the real world and virtual reality.
- Manipulation – there are adequate controls which are easy to manipulate particularly in a mobile environment.
- Perception – Design must enable user to quickly perceive displays even when mobile. So displays should be easy to navigate and simple.

Outside offices and buildings, an attractive option for a user to have access to a computer interface is through wearables. There are challenges however that need to be addressed to fulfill the tasks in terms of contextual awareness, interface, adaptation to tasks, and cognitive model. These include:

- **Modalities of Input/output** – the ease of use and accuracy of modalities developed that try to copy the human brain's input/output capacity are not yet satisfactory. Frustrations bedevil users when there are inaccuracies. Also the computing requirement of these modalities is way beyond what low-weight wearable devices have. Input devices which are simple to use are needed.

- **Models of User interface** – there is a need for extensive experimentation in using applications involving end-users.

- **Capability-applications matching** – evaluation and design of interface should prioritize development of most effective way to access information and avoid creating additional features.

- **Simple methodology in interface evaluation** – current evaluation approaches are too complicated and time-consuming making them unsuitable in interface design. What is needed is an evaluation methodology that addresses frustration and human errors.

- **Context awareness** – for context aware computing to be realized, several questions must be answered. These include application models that integrate the social and cognitive aspects, social and cognitive mapping of inputs from many sensors, anticipating the needs of users, and interacting with the users.

Conclusion

Thank you again for purchasing this book!

I hope this book was able to help you to gain useful knowledge and understanding about human-computer interaction.

The next step is to apply what you have learned.

Finally, if you enjoyed this book, please take the time to share your thoughts and post a review on Amazon. It'd be greatly appreciated!

Thank you and good luck!

www.ingramcontent.com/pod-product-compliance
Lightning Source LLC
Chambersburg PA
CBHW070843070326
40690CB00009B/1677